KU-713-960

Learning on the Net

A Practical Guide to Enhancing Learning in Primary Classrooms

Alan Pritchard

David Fulton Publishers

David Fulton Publishers Ltd
The Chiswick Centre, 414 Chiswick High Road, London W4 5TF

www.fultonpublishers.co.uk

First published in Great Britain in 2004 by David Fulton Publishers.

10 9 8 7 6 5 4 3 2 1

Note: The right of the author to be identified as the author of this work has been asserted by him in accordance with the Copyright, Designs and Patents Act 1988.

David Fulton Publishers is a division of Granada Learning Limited, part of the ITV plc.

Copyright © Alan Pritchard 2004

British Library Cataloguing in Publication Data
A catalogue record for this book is available from the British Library.

ISBN 1 84312 082 8

All rights reserved. No part of this publication may be reproduced, stored in a retrieval system or transmitted, in any form or by any means, electronic, mechanical, photocopying, or otherwise, without the prior permission of the publishers.

Typeset by Servis Filmsetting Ltd, Manchester
Printed and bound in Great Britain

00190217

Tower Hamlets Schools Library Service
Tower Hamlets Professional Development Centre
English Street, London E3 4TA
Tel: 0171 364 6428

Contents

Dedicated to my family and to all of the colleagues, children and students who have shaped my attitudes and understandings over the many years since I began teaching, especially Jackie, Maria and Frances who have shaped me and loved me, as I love them.

Introduction

It is fair to say that technology has changed the face of our world. Almost everything around us relies, to some extent, upon technology. Not just technology but *information technology* has had, and is having, a big impact on our lives. To use the most recent terminology in the field of education and computers, it is *information and communications technology* (ICT) that is having such a big impact on all of us. When our gas meter is read, a hand-held device downloads our details to the main computer back at base. Our bank accounts are computerised; we can shop via the Internet; problems with our cars can be diagnosed by computer; any number of machines and devices in our homes rely on microchips; the staggering array of facilities contained within the tiniest mobile phone just seems to grow and grow;and much of the world of medicine would be virtually unrecognisable to the practitioners of earlier years. There are many more examples too.

If ICTs have changed, and continue to change, the face of everyday life then it is obvious that these changes will spill over into classrooms. Anyone who knows even the smallest amount about contemporary schools will know that this is the case. Twenty years ago some enthusiastic teachers chose to introduce the computers which were then available into their classrooms. BBC, Sinclair and Research Machines computers were all to be found in schools, though only in small numbers at first. Now, in the early years of the 21st century, the element of choice concerning computer use has disappeared and ICT is an established and legally required feature of our schools. The National Curriculum includes ICT as a subject in its own right and the other subjects of the National Curriculum all have their own requirements related to the ways in which the use of one type or another of hardware, software, or access to the Internet, might be included in the range of experiences offered to children. There is a clear unequivocal expectation that teachers will use ICTs in teaching, and that all pupils will have a breadth of experience with ICTs during the years of compulsory schooling.

For the purposes of the National Curriculum, Information and Communication Technology is to:

> *. . . refer to the range of tools and techniques relating to computer-based hardware and software; to communications including both directed and broadcast; to information sources such as CD-ROM and the Internet, and to associated technologies such as robots, video-conferencing, and digital TV.* (The National Curriculum: DfEE, QCA 1999a)

It can be seen, then, that when referring to ICTs, a wide range of different devices and machines is being considered. However, the most common machine or device found in schools is the standard computer, whether a laptop, a stand-alone desktop, or a networked machine.

The National Curriculum includes a statement on the use of ICT across the curriculum. The statement is short and included here in full:

Use of Information and Communication Technology Across the Curriculum

1. *Pupils should be given opportunities to apply and develop their ICT capability through the use of ICT tools to support their learning in all subjects (with the exception of physical education at Key Stages 1 and 2).*

2. *Pupils should be given opportunities to support their work by being taught to:*

a) *find things out from a variety of sources, selecting and synthesising the information to meet their needs and developing an ability to question its accuracy, bias and plausibility*

b) *develop their ideas using ICT tools to amend and refine their work and enhance its quality and accuracy*

c) *exchange and share information, both directly and through electronic media*

d) *review, modify and evaluate their work, reflecting critically on its quality, as it progresses.*

(DfEE, QCA 1999a)

The strands of skills, knowledge and understanding in the ICT National Curriculum, give an emphasis to the use of ICT as a support for learning in subjects, rather than ICT for its own ends. The strands are:

- finding things out;
- developing ideas and making things happen;
- exchanging and sharing information; and
- reviewing, modifying and evaluating work as it progresses.

The programmes of study also allow for a developing understanding of ICT, which is found in the section headed *Breadth of Study Across the Key Stage*. This breadth is to be supported by:

- the uses of ICT inside and outside school (Key Stage One);
- trying out different ways of obtaining, developing, exchanging and presenting information (Key Stage Two);

- (further) exploring a variety of information sources, ICT tools and applications (Key Stage Three);
- tackling demanding problems in a variety of contexts (Key Stage Four).

The programmes of study have a focus on finding and making use of information in subject contexts. The emphasis is on making effective use of the available technologies for the increase of subject knowledge, the growth of understanding and the development of skills. It is important to realise that the purpose of seeking out information is not solely for the increase of knowledge, though this is an element of the work. Whether it is gleaned from the Internet, CD-ROM, or gathered via a sensor in the classroom, information should also be used to increase understanding. The theme of 'converting information into understanding', will be developed later and will run through all of this book.

The statutory requirements for ICT are clear. They present a coherent and supportive framework for making effective use of the technologies across the curriculum. There can be little doubt that the use of ICTs in general, and the Internet in particular, must form an important part of every child's experience in school.

The use of the Internet in education has become an issue for many teachers. This applies across the age phases and across all subjects. It is recognised that the Internet 'has a lot to offer', but it is not always clear, in a variety of different age and subject contexts, just how to make best advantage of what there is on offer.

Over the years, the use of computers in classrooms has presented a range of problems. Many of these problems will be familiar: unreliable hardware and software; uncertainty about appropriate teaching approaches; lack of clear organisational strategies; unproductive use of inappropriate software, and so on. Now with more experience and greatly improved facilities, with improved software, and new approaches to making use of older software, educational practice with computers is improving. There is also a growing evidence base from research that the well-planned use of computer-based teaching can reap learning benefits for pupils across the range of school subjects (see for example, University of Newcastle upon Tyne Department of Education 1999; ImaCT2 2001).

One problem persists, however, and this is the problem of how to make best use of the Internet in teaching. This is not to say that there is not good practice which leads to very good results, but in many cases the incredibly large amount of information, and the diverse possibilities for activity and interaction, are not used to best effect.

In this book the possibilities for effective use of information from the Internet and other electronic sources will be highlighted and developed. We will consider in detail the ways that the wealth of resources, which include a range of activity-based and interactive sites, can be of value in well-planned teaching situations.

We can divide the main areas of work that can be affected positively by well-planned use of the Internet into three broad fields.

Literacy. Using texts to help learning in different subjects at different levels; including dialogue with others. This can be in the context of literacy learning, i.e., learning about language and literature, but it is also most certainly in the context of other subjects too. We must not forget that literacy can be developed through work in other subjects, and that learning in other subjects benefits from well-developed literacy skills.

Numeracy. The use of numbers and number activities from the Internet can be in the context of maths/numeracy, and there can also be the use of numbers/statistics in many other subject contexts. As with literacy, the effective use of numbers can lead to advances in learning and understanding in a range of subjects.

Science. Activities with simulations and dynamic representations, facts and figures, sensing (making use of 'real' data), all have the potential to assist in the process of developing understanding of scientific, and other, concepts. Many science-based resources can be used and further explored with the use of spreadsheets and databases.

These three areas will be explored in the following chapters and examples in the form of short case studies will exemplify approaches which can be taken. The layout of the book will be in terms of:

- using words;
- using numbers and number activities;
- other resources.

These *other resources* are in many ways the most interesting since in some cases they are the most different from traditional classroom resources. These other resources include words, sounds, pictures, both moving and static, and combinations of all of these, but they also encompass new opportunities for interactivity and communication that have not previously been so readily available or so well developed technologically. There will not be a strict delineation of subject boundaries and the given examples will straddle the subjects of the curriculum. The case studies will cover a range of National Curriculum subjects and will be taken from both Key Stages One and Two.

First we will look in detail at the Internet, its history and make-up, and some of its inherent difficulties. We will also look broadly at the notion of learning, particularly in the context of pupils' work with information and activity mediated by the Internet or other electronic sources. Many teachers in in-service training and in study for higher degrees, have shown interest in learning the theory and principles put forward in this book, while at the same time bemoaning the paucity of their experience during initial teacher training in terms of introductions to the basic tenets of the major learning theories influencing practice in classrooms today. Chapter Two seeks to supply background knowledge of learning theory.

This background will be helpful when teachers are working towards understanding fully approaches to teaching and learning with the Internet, and associated sources of information and activity, which they are faced with developing and using.

The aim of this book is not to produce a list of approved websites and prescribed activities. It is more a set of ideas and principles, with examples, set in the context of what is known about learning and effective practice in schools, which can be applied and tailored by creative teachers in a wide range of subject- and age-related contexts. Since websites occasionally disappear without warning, it is not always useful to set out the detailed use of specific elements of particular sites. However, some very good sites for classroom use have been available for some time and give every impression of remaining for some time to come. All of the sites referred to in the text were fully operational, and as described, at the time of writing. In any case, the principles remain the same, and the activities can be used and improved upon in other website contexts.

CHAPTER 1

The Internet – what's it all about?

The Internet is a very large computer network that is made up from other smaller networks of computers. Networks of computers can be very large or can consist of just two machines linked together. The Internet is actually made up of millions of computers that are connected in a multitude of different configurations and which, through the vast array of connections provided by the worldwide telecommunications system, can make connections with each other and transfer many different kinds of information. The telecommunications system that the Internet makes use of consists of the underground cables and overhead wires, the exchanges, the satellite links and sometimes radio links that have been developed over many years by the many different international, national and local authorities and companies.

The Internet network of computers making a worldwide community, runs into millions of 'members', and the number of computers that have the capability to connect with the network runs into many more millions. The Internet holds a vast store of information with great possibilities for education.

The World Wide Web (WWW) is, in a sense, the visible face of the Internet. The WWW is the interface between users and the network of computers where the many millions of websites with their many millions of items of information are to be found.

The Internet offers a range of facilities, allowing users to obtain information and resources, to communicate and to publish information. The World Wide Web provides relatively straightforward access to the vast quantity of information and resources available on the Internet and is the facility that people use to 'surf' for information. The Internet is made up of millions of 'pages', of information. The collection of pages created by one individual or organisation is known as a website. Each page can include text, images, sound, animation and video and has its own unique address.

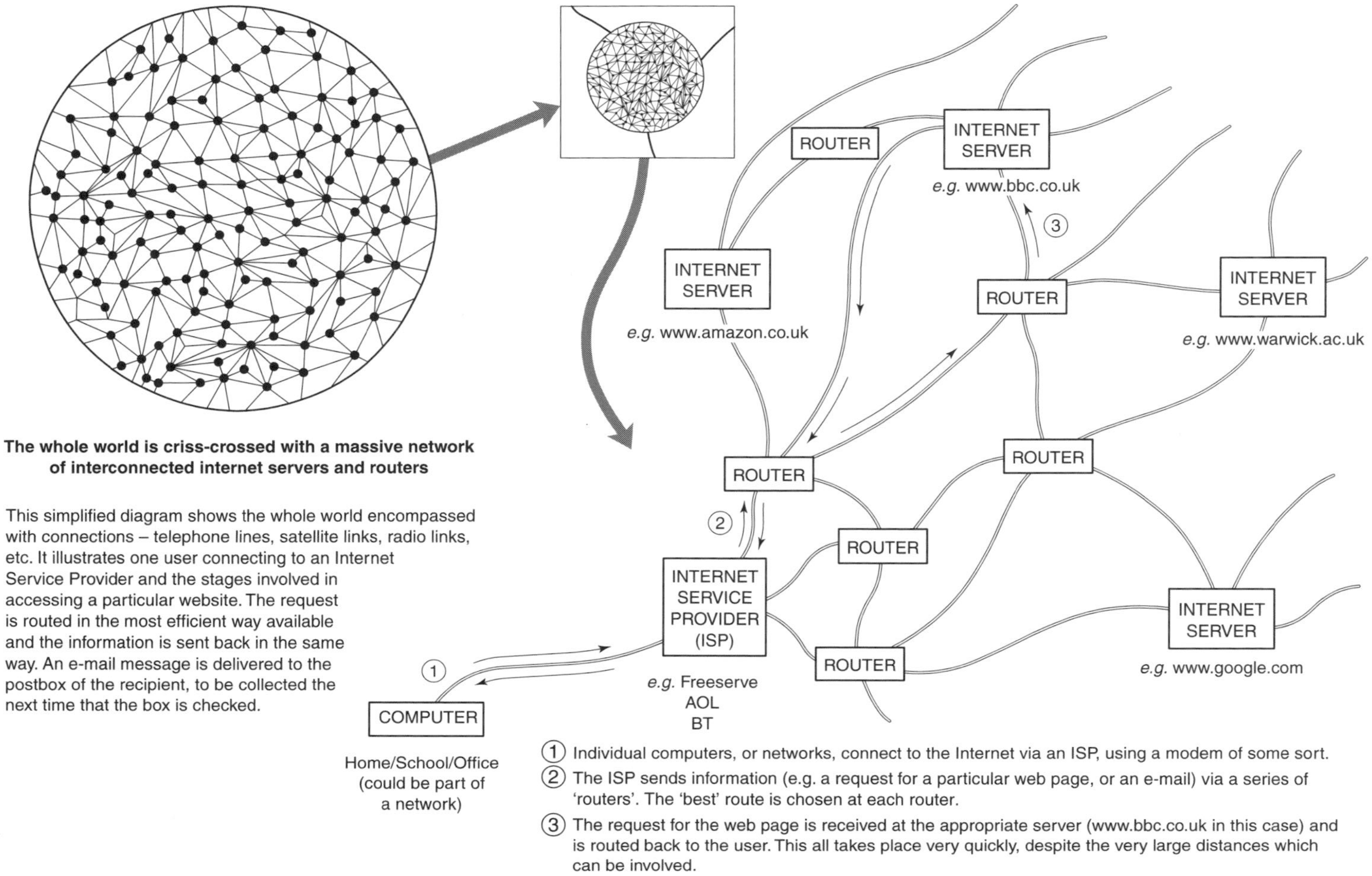
The whole world is criss-crossed with a massive network of interconnected internet servers and routers
This simplified diagram shows the whole world encompassed with connections – telephone lines, satellite links, radio links, etc. It illustrates one user connecting to an Internet Service Provider and the stages involved in accessing a particular website. The request is routed in the most efficient way available and the information is sent back in the same way. An e-mail message is delivered to the postbox of the recipient, to be collected the next time that the box is checked.
ROUTER
INTERNET SERVER
e.g. www.bbc.co.uk
INTERNET SERVER
e.g. www.amazon.co.uk
3
ROUTER
INTERNET SERVER
e.g. www.warwick.ac.uk
ROUTER
ROUTER
2
ROUTER
INTERNET SERVICE PROVIDER (ISP)
1
INTERNET SERVER
ROUTER
e.g. www.google.com
e.g. Freeserve
AOL
BT
COMPUTER
Home/School/Office (could be part of a network)
1 Individual computers, or networks, connect to the Internet via an ISP, using a modem of some sort.
2 The ISP sends information (e.g. a request for a particular web page, or an e-mail) via a series of 'routers'. The 'best' route is chosen at each router.
3 The request for the web page is received at the appropriate server (www.bbc.co.uk in this case) and is routed back to the user. This all takes place very quickly, despite the very large distances which can be involved.

Figure 1.1 *Worldwide connections*

Web Addresses: Uniform Resource Locator (URL)

Though the addresses of websites sometimes appear as a jumble of letters and numbers, there is, as we would expect, a simple logic to the way that they are constructed. An analogy with a simple postal address can be made.

Table 1.1 The elements of a website address

http://www.cavern-liverpool.co.uk/mmt/combo.htm			
	Address for the Internet	**What does this mean?**	**Address for an item of mail**
What is it?	http://	Hypertext transfer protocol: one of the different ways in which information can be transmitted over the Internet.	Letter, parcel or telegram
Where is it going?	www.cavern-liverpool	The World Wide Web server for Cavern Tours, a company in Liverpool dedicated to the Beatles' Liverpool; organisers of various tours.	Country and city
Additional information	.co.uk/	A commercial, i.e. a profit-making, organisation in the United Kingdom	
More precisely?	mmt/	A part of the Cavern Tours server with information about Magical Mystery Tours	District, road name and number
Final destination?	combo.htm	A document which is called 'combo' and contains information about a set of combined tours visiting various famous Liverpool locations	Name of person

We can see that the particular page displayed at the address above gives details of the range of tours around places in Liverpool frequented by the Beatles in days gone by. Virtually all Internet addresses are made up of the components above, though there are some less frequently encountered exceptions.

Certain parts of a web address can give clues to the location and ownership of the site in question. For example 'ac.uk' tells the users that the site is located in an academic institution in the United Kingdom. More consideration of the probable location, ownership and reliability of websites which can be deduced from their addresses will be made in a later section dealing with website evaluation.

A Brief History

The Advanced Research Projects Agency (ARPA), an arm of the United States Government working mainly on defence-related technological developments, is where it all began. In 1969 ARPRANET was established as a way of setting up communication between computers in different locations around the United States. This was seen as a way of sharing research ideas and data between universities, but it soon became clear to those working on the project that the implications for military command and control were far-reaching. This first network was 'distributed', rather than being arranged as a hub with 'spokes' (see Figures 1.2 and 1.3). This means that a very large number of different routes on the network from any given point to another can be found, instead of there being just one route which could easily be disrupted, by an enemy or by a technical difficulty, for example.

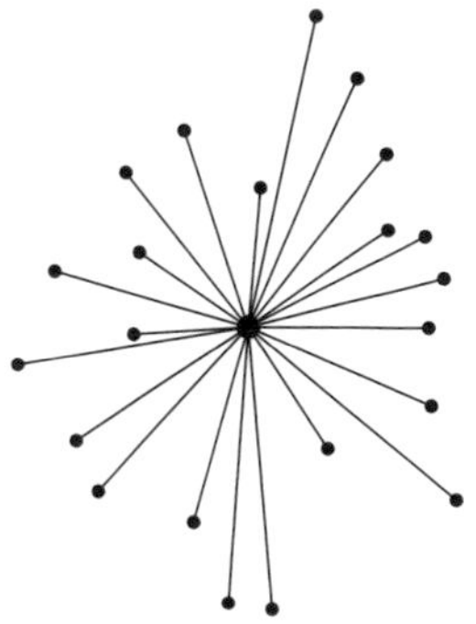

Figure 1.2 *A network made up of a hub with spokes*

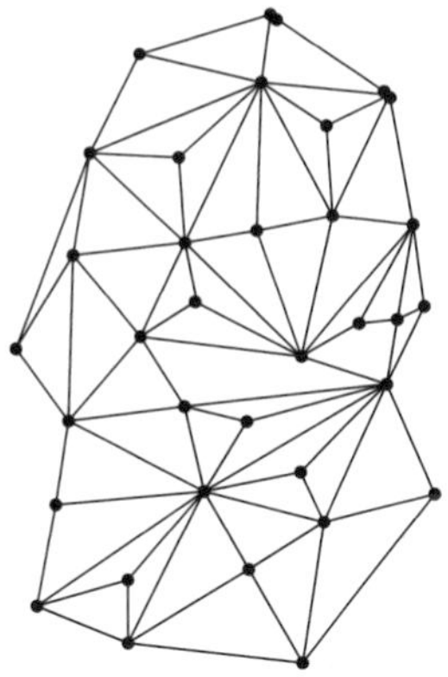

Figure 1.3 *A distributed network*

By 1991 the World Wide Web, invented by Tim Berners-Lee as a means of simplifying the exchange of large amounts of data concerning particle physics, became available to those who were able to equip themselves with a modem. A modem is a device which can be connected simultaneously to a computer and to a telephone system and used to convert information from a computer into a form that can be transmitted via the telephone system's infrastructure.

One definition, picked from the results list of an Internet search, of the World Wide Web, and there are many to chose from, is:

> *'wide-area hypermedia information retrieval initiative aiming to give universal access to a large universe of documents.'*

This can be enlarged upon as follows:

Wide-area

The World Wide Web spans the whole globe.

Hypermedia

It contains a range of media, including text, pictures, sound and video. The individual elements are connected by hyperlinks which connect pages to one another and allow for swift movement from one location to another.

Information Retrieval

Viewing a web document is very easy thanks to the help of web browsers, which are the point of contact between the user and the web. Web browsers allow the user to retrieve pages just by clicking a mouse button when the pointer on the screen is over a *link*, or by entering appropriate web addresses. Information may be retrieved from the web extremely quickly, by any suitably set up computer with an Internet connection.

Universal Access

No matter what type of computer is being used, or what type of computer the information is held on, web browsers allow for apparently seamless connection to, and movement between, many different computer locations.

Large Universe of Documents

Anyone can publish a web page. No matter what obscure information you want to find, there is bound to be someone who has produced and published a web page about it. It will not necessarily be exactly what you want, it might not be accurate or written in an appropriate style, but it will be there. There are many millions of web pages in existence now, and many more are being added each day. (The importance of evaluating web-based resources will be dealt with later.)

The Relationship between the WWW and the Internet

The World Wide Web is just one of the services that the Internet provides. It is the best known and probably the most widely used. To all intents and purposes the World Wide Web is the public face of the Internet. It is the interface between users and the complex, but hidden, structure which allows the Internet to function and which is a mystery to most users. There is no real need for the mystery to be solved for most of us, but a little knowledge and understanding can sometimes help when making use of the facilities provided. This is similar to the notion that in order to drive a car, a driver must fully understand the finer details of the workings of all of its systems. This is not the case, but a little knowledge may well be of use.

Some other services provided by the Internet are e-mail, FTP, usenet, newsgroups and mailing lists, chat rooms and video conferencing.

E-mail

This allows users to send and receive written messages via a telephone line. Children use e-mail in school for communicating with pen pals, to send questions to experts, to help with project work and to swap information about their locality with children in other countries, for example.

FTP (File Transfer Protocol)

This is a way to transfer files from computer to computer on the Internet. You might typically use it to transfer a web page from your computer (where you are writing it) to a web server so it can be accessed by the world, or you may use it to download a file from a public archive. There are many FTP clients (programs) available. Most Internet users work very efficiently without having to know about FTP.

Usenet (also called Internet News)

This is a huge network of discussion groups. Newsgroups are like noticeboards where people log into a particular group to read and contribute remarks or questions. There are thousands of newsgroups covering any and every topic and interest. The groups are set up within broad categories such as sci (science), biz (business), comp (computers), soc (society) and alt (alternate). For each broad category there are a great many more specific titles.

Mailing Lists

These usually consist of a group of people who exchange e-mail about a subject that interests them. For instance, a mailing list called 'uk-schools' allows people with an interest in computers in education to write to the list about relevant topics, alert one another to useful websites or ask for help and advice.

Chat Rooms

These allow a number of people to 'meet' on the Internet and have live, text-based conversations in what is known as 'real-time'. It is similar to having a telephone conversation with one or a number of people, except that the participants type instead of talk. Individual websites, such as the BBC (http://www.bbc.co.uk/education/schools/) and the Science Museum (http://www.nmsi.ac.uk/education/webcast1.html) are increasingly setting up specific times for question and answer sessions with subject experts or well-known personalities. Other facilities allow for social chat. Some chat rooms are unrestricted and unmonitored whereas the more reputable chat rooms have controls both in the hands of the users – in that they can block contact from specified users – and in the hands of a chat room moderator who can make checks for content-related matters.

Video Conferencing

This enables two or more people, in different locations, to talk to one another while also being able to see each other. It is also possible to arrange for the exchange of audio, video, images or any other digital file to allow users in different places to work simultaneously on the same document. Secondary schools, in particular, have used video conferences as a resource, for foreign language learning, for example.

Information and Communication

The make-up of the Internet can be divided crudely into two broad categories: information and communication. Beneath each of these headings there are, naturally, subdivisions. Information can be *accessed*, or *published*, and communication can in general terms be of two different types: *synchronous*, happening at the same time – that is the people communicating are actually sitting and responding to messages as they are written (known as *chatting)* and *asynchronous*, where messages are written and sent but not necessarily read or responded to until later – e-mail is an example of this.

The World Wide Web, and the other areas of the Internet above, can be classified into one of these headings. WWW viewing is clearly concerned with access to information or, when used to create pages and sites, to publishing information. E-mail is asynchronous communication, whereas video conferencing is synchronous. Pachler and Williams (Pachler and Williams 1999) draw out the distinctions between different Internet uses and describe what they call the *Internet tools* which are used for the different activities.

Internet Use in Schools

The Internet, by means of the World Wide Web, and initially by the use of elementary e-mail systems, has become the latest in a list of technological advances to be introduced into classrooms. In the early to mid-1990s to use the Internet in a primary school setting was to take a bold move into the unknown. At first access was slow and unreliable and the Internet was only a place for the real enthusiasts to visit. To make use of the Internet in school was not a particularly obvious option to follow. Certainly information could be sought out for use in class time, but to rely on the system, which was actually quite expensive at first, to provide access for the duration of a lesson, was asking a little too much. The use of e-mail was introduced experimentally, and in some schools contact was made, sometimes only locally, with other classes. Examples of contact between more remote locations at home and abroad soon came to light. As the availability and reliability of the equipment increased, so did the opportunities for teachers to try out some of the new communications-based activities.

Official figures from the UK Government give a picture of the current position as far as schools with Internet access is concerned: in 2002 more than 99 per cent of all primary schools had access to the Internet. This is of course a crude measure, because it gives no indication of the use to which the Internet connection is put. However it does show an incredible increase over the preceding few years.

Table 1.2 Primary schools: net connection

	1998	1999	2000	2001	2002
Percentage of Primary schools connected to the Internet	17	62	86	96	>99

Despite all of this, it is important to remember that: 'The Internet is a generally unregulated environment. There is a wide range of material available covering virtually every aspect of our life or activity, much of it positive, some of it offensive' (DfEE 1999). As well as being very large and generally of a positive nature another aspect of the make-up of the Internet which must be held firmly in mind is that a very large proportion of the Internet is attempting to sell to the, sometimes unsuspecting, surfer.

Through the Internet, children are able to 'visit' places and take part in events that would otherwise be too far away, or too costly. For example, the 24-Hour Museum enables visitors to take a virtual tour, the Hubble Space Telescope offers full-colour pictures of planets, while the Whole Brain Atlas gives access to colour MRI scan images of the entire brain. Other sites are specifically designed to support education in the UK, such as the National Grid for Learning (NGfL) which offers pupils, teachers and parents access to a growing collection of good quality curriculum-rich resources and educational support material. Searching for information on the Web can help pupils to develop information handling skills. The Internet is an ideal vehicle for introducing pupils to, and illustrating, concepts such as audience and purpose, authorship and bias. By viewing sites with opposing views, notions of subjectivity/objectivity, fact/opinion and overt/covert bias can be demonstrated in an 'immediate' and powerful way.

The Internet is a remarkable resource to have access to, but it must be used with appropriate caution, and with due attention to the safeguards set out below.

Difficulties which arise when using the Internet

Undesirable Material

Sadly there is a propensity amongst the human race to dwell on the unsavoury. A dislike, in the western world at least, for censorship means that a considerable amount of what many would consider inappropriate and undesirable material is regularly and increasingly posted onto Internet sites by individuals and companies who are eager to 'exploit the marketplace'. Pornography is apparently rife; extreme political views, sometimes extolling the virtues of violence are present; instructions for building bombs or concocting poisons are also to be found. This is to mention but a few undesirable examples of what exists on the virtual platform of the Internet.

The sites where these items are to be found are not always easy to identify, but with simple searches they can be found and this is a cause for serious concern amongst many parents and those responsible for the well-being of children in schools, in particular. Apart from vigilance, there are some simple and effective steps which can be take to avoid situations where children are inadvertently exposed to inappropriate content, or even driven to seek it out through a sense of misplaced excitement or curiosity. Occasionally, on an unprotected Internet connected computer, it is possible to stumble upon the sort of material outlined here. The systems listed below make this very much less likely to happen, but will also allow teachers the freedom to make full use of the rich source of activity and information which the Internet provides.

Safeguards When Using the Internet

Filtering Systems

Filtering systems are designed to prevent user access to unsuitable material. When the filtering system is turned on it is not possible to visit sites that the system has been configured to recognise as unsuitable. It is possible to add or remove certain features of websites that will then be recognised as either allowable or not allowable. Although useful, filtering systems are not always foolproof.

Walled Gardens

Walled gardens are services that offer those who make use of them limited access to pre-selected and approved websites. Walled gardens offer a very high level of control and protection over what can and cannot be accessed and also against the intentional or inadvertent accessing of inappropriate material. Some Internet

Service Providers (ISPs) and some Local Education Authorities offer this service to school and home users.

Firewalls

Firewalls are security systems that are designed to prevent unauthorised access to or from a private network and provide security control that enables sites to connect safely to other networks. For example a firewall could prevent school users accessing any sites that fall outside of the established school/local authority approved network. Firewalls come in the form of either hardware or software, or they can be a combination of both. Firewalls can be set up to cater for individual requirements.

Monitoring Organisations and Systems

Some organisations, such as the Internet Watch Foundation, and Childnet International, Gridwatch and Safe Surf, operate systems that monitor Internet content and ensure that users do not stray into unsuitable areas of the Internet. The National Grid for Learning in the UK, also has a monitoring role. These systems, when operated, monitor and detect certain unsuitable sites and documents, and prevent access to them.

Internet Acceptable Use Policies and Contracts

An Acceptable Use Policy is a document, signed by pupils and their parents, guardians or carers, detailing the ways in which the Internet should be used. The policy needs to balance the usefulness of being able to exploit the potential of Internet resources for educational purposes including communication, with safeguards against unacceptable activity.

More information about this important aspect of Internet use can be found at the UK's National Grid for Learning Superhighway Safety Site at: http://safety.ngfl.gov.uk/ukonline/.

In summary, the following 'common-sense' approach to Internet use can be used in schools, to help to establish safe use:

- site computers in public places where everyone can see what is on the screen;
- take an interest in the Internet and regularly discuss what young people see and use;
- be fully aware of what projects children are undertaking on the Internet;
- monitor on-line time and investigate incidences of excessive hours spent on the Internet;
- educate pupils to use the Internet in a safe, sensible and responsible manner;
- encourage pupils to become critical users of the Internet;

- warn youngsters that there are unsavoury sites on the Internet and discuss the issues involved;
- set up a reporting system so that pupils know what to do if they find unsuitable material;
- make it a matter of policy that all pupils sign a code of conduct and consider sending copies to parents for them to sign;
- make it clear that the misuse of the Internet will not be taken lightly.

Too Much Information

There is no question that the Internet contains more information than anyone could possibly ever wish to consult. In order to make effective use of information from the Internet, first it has to be located, and secondly it has, in one way or another, to be verified as useful. This leads to questions first about searching, and secondly to questions concerning the importance of evaluating web-based resources quickly and effectively.

Searching, and Otherwise Locating Information

A simple search on a topic of interest can lead to a list containing so many Internet sites that it is virtually impossible to deal with. For example, a search using Google (www.google.com), a well-known and respected Internet search engine, looking for information concerning fitness produces a list of 19,900,000 sites in less than 1 second, a great many of which are designed to encourage the hapless surfer to buy products designed to improve the fitness of the human body beyond recognition. Clearly in an educational setting, when basic research dealing with the introductory notions of the importance of cardiovascular fitness for a happy and healthy life is being undertaken, this is very unhelpful.

Dealing with what has been termed *information overload* is a very real problem, both in schools and elsewhere. As we will see later there are ways in which the volume of information which is located via the Internet can be decreased and the relevance of it to the user increased. Indeed, much of what comes later in this book will set out strategies for Internet use that have the aim of easing the burden of having too much information to deal with.

Website Evaluation

It is never too soon to encourage young Internet users to consider the value, integrity and usefulness of a website. Simple questions such as 'Is this what we are looking for?' can focus the attention of a newcomer to the Internet on the veracity of the resource in question.

We will consider the evaluation of websites in some detail here, as it is a very important aspect of Internet use, and it is possible for teachers to introduce skills which can lead to the discerning use of the Internet from a very early age. Firstly let us look at different aspects of web-based resources which have a bearing on the style and quality of the site and then consider how to approach the evaluation of websites in the primary school setting.

There is a list of website attributes, concerning the quality of any particular site, which is widely quoted, both on official websites and in other reputable locations. (For example, the UK Government site 'Superhighway Safety', hosted by the Department for Education and Skills, can be found at: http://stagesafety.ngfl.gov.uk/schools/). The list of attributes is included below.

- authority
- purpose
- audience
- relevance
- objectivity
- accuracy
- currency
- format
- links

These headings are enlarged upon below (the heading 'Ease of Use' has been added) by means of sets of questions which might be posed in order to establish more information about a particular site and to enable an evaluation based on more than initial impressions. Some of the questions are taken from the same source.

Authority

Who has written the information?
What is the authority or expertise of the author?
Are there contact details for the author?
Where does the content originate from?
Is it clear who the author is and who has published the site?
Are they qualified to provide information on this topic?
Is the material biased?
Where is the content published?
What is the domain name of the website?
Is it published by a large organisation, or on a personal website?
Does the website cover the topic fully?
Does it provide links and references to other materials?

If links to other materials are provided, are these evaluated or annotated to provide further information? Do these links work?
Does the site contain any advertising?
Does any advertising influence the content?

Purpose, audience and relevance

What are the aims of the site?
Does it achieve its aims?
Who is the intended audience for this content?
Is the content easy to read and understand?
Is the site specifically aimed at children?
If so, is the level and tone of the content appropriate?
Is the site specifically aimed at adults?
Is the site relevant to me?
Does the material provide everything that is needed?
Could more relevant material be found elsewhere, in a book or magazine for example?
Is the site trying to sell something?

Objectivity

Is the information offered as fact or opinion?
Is the information biased in any obvious way?

Accuracy and Currency

Does the information appear to be accurate?
Are additional references given?
Can the information be verified from other sources?
Is the spelling and grammar correct?
Is the content dated?
When was the content last updated?
Are all links up to date and valid?
Are any areas of the site 'under construction'?

Format

Does the site contain information in the format that I want?

Links

Does the site give me advice/ideas/other choices?

Ease of Use

Is the site easy to use?
Is the site well structured?
Is it easy to find relevant information?

Is the content in an easy-to-use format?
What facilities does the site provide to help locate information?
Does it have a search facility?
Is the menu navigation logical?
Does it provide a site map or index?
Does the site load quickly?
Is the site attractive in design?
Is the content copyright, or can it be used providing the source is acknowledged?

These questions are all pertinent, and certainly deserving of attention. Experienced Internet users often run through these points, or at least some of them, when they visit a site for the first time. As they are phrased here, they are not suitable for use directly by children, but it is possible to introduce the ideas and skills involved in ways which primary-aged children can understand. A simple sheet to fill in can be used to encourage children to think about the issues. This need not be done as a regular feature of work with the Internet, but can be very useful as a way of introducing the process. Some teachers keep a bank of website evaluations, or mini-reviews, prepared by children as resources for others.

Something as simple as the example below might well suffice in some situations:

Table 1.3 From Richmond Hill Education Action Zone

Website name	Web Address	Comments

In other cases, where more detail would better serve the purpose, a sheet designed around a set of questions could be used. The questions, which are obviously open to change and interpretation, should be worded appropriately and could include:

1. Is it clear who has written the information?
2. Are the aims of the site clear?
3. Does the site achieve its aims?
4. Is the site relevant to me?
5. Can the information be checked?
6. When was the site produced?
7. Is the information biased in any way?
8. Does the site take a long time to load?
9. Is the site attractive?

There are many Internet resources to help with the evaluation of websites. A keyword search on any search engine will provide a range of sites, and some useful tools and checklists. Jan Alexander and Marsha Ann Tate of the Wolfgram Memorial Library in the US have produced a useful set of resources, including a copyright-free presentation which covers the main criteria for evaluating web resources. The ICT advice site provides guidance on evaluating and reviewing websites, including some key considerations for teachers (http://ictadvice.org.uk).

The National Grid for Learning (www.ngfl.gov.uk) provides a gateway to educational resources on the Internet, through a network of selected links to websites that offer high quality content and information. It also provides links to web-based resources that can assist with evaluating websites.

QUICK – the Quality Information Checklist which was developed by a group within the UK National Health Service, aims to help teachers and pupils evaluate health information on the Internet for use in the classroom. The list can of course be used in the context of any topic, and provides very good resources for this type of work (www.quick.org.uk/).

An important pointer to the pedigree of a website, and a means of answering some of the questions above, can be found in its address (URL). As we saw earlier, certain elements of a web address give detail of its location. The example given was that an address which includes the characters '.ac.uk' has its source in a British academic institution, usually a university. The tables below gives details of other elements of web addresses which give insight into their background and ownership.

Table 1.4 A selection of top-level domain codes and their meanings

Domain Code	Meaning
.co	Commercial body in the UK. Used almost exclusively in the form '.co.uk'
.com	Originally intended for 'commercial' bodies, but any person or organisation, commercial or otherwise, may register and use .com
.edu	Educational institutions. Mostly used in the USA and Australia.
.gov	Government departments, agencies and branches. Including local authorities.
.mil	Military bodies.
.net	Bodies and computers that represent part of the Internet's infrastructure.
.nhs.uk	UK National Health Service trust or department.
.org	Designated for miscellaneous bodies that do not fit under any of the other top-level domains. Mostly used by non-profit organisations.

Table 1.5 A selection of country domain codes. There is a code for every country in the world

Country Code	Country
.au	Australia
.br	Brazil
.ch	Switzerland
.cn	China
.de	Germany
.fr	France
.jp	Japan
.uk	United Kingdom
.us	United States of America – this is very often missing, since the very first web addresses were from the USA.

Chapter Summary

- the Internet is very large, and growing rapidly;
- the Internet contains enormous quantities of resources which can be very useful to teachers and pupils alike;
- there are dangers associated with Internet use, but there are ways of protecting against them;
- the skills of website evaluation are important and should be approached at an early stage in children's experience.

CHAPTER 2

Learning – what is it and how do we make it more effective?

It may seem a little out of place in a book that is ostensibly dealing with the Internet, to include a chapter that summarises recent and current thinking about learning. There is, however, good reason for this. A basic understanding of processes of learning is probably essential for those who intend to develop activities which will have the potential to lead to effective learning. In more recent times there has been a reduction in the emphasis given to learning about 'learning' from a theoretical standpoint, in initial courses for teacher education. This has been for a variety of reasons. For example, there has been a proliferation of regulations from central government which has made great demands on the training providers, and squeezed the time available for teaching, substantially. There has also been an emergence of alternative entry routes into teaching; some of which can be called 'work-based'. This too has led to a reduction of the time available for theoretical work. To be fair, the balance between practice and theory has been improved, but this has been at the expense of some areas of teaching that have traditionally made up the curriculum for initial training courses. For this reason, and because of the inherent importance of learning theory to classroom practice, a section dealing with this key element of a teacher's knowledge base has been included.

In very general terms there are two branches of the psychology of learning that have made important inroads into the practice of teaching in past decades. First there is behaviourism, and secondly constructivism. Both of these branches have a series of sub-branches, but it is reasonably fair to divide learning theory in this way. As we will see, behaviourism is concerned with what can be seen happening – behaviour; constructivism rests on the idea that knowledge, and more importantly, understanding, is constructed by individual learners.

Taking each in turn, we will explore the notions of the two branches of theory, spending less time on the more dated and generally less well-favoured branch of behaviourism, and consider the implications of the theory for work which is undertaken with, and relies upon, the Internet.

Behaviourist, or Stimulus–Response Theories

In looking at the ways in which learning can be encouraged from sources such as the Internet, the theory of behaviourism is not the most important of the range of theories that may have something to offer to teachers and learners alike. We will see that the underpinning principles of behaviourism come to the fore in one or two instances but, for the most part, it is the realm of constructivist psychology that plays the greatest part in our consideration of theoretical perspectives. As a starting point, because there are occasions in learning activities when behaviourism dominates, and also for the sake of completeness, it is interesting to take an overview of what behaviourism stands for and where it came from. Looking at behaviourism will also give a point of reference against which the notions of constructive learning might be measured and compared.

Behaviourism is based around the central notion of the reaction made by the 'learner' to a particular stimulus. In simplistic terms, for example, a performing lion in a circus responds to a particular stimulus, the crack of a whip, by roaring and raising itself up on two legs. In a classroom situation, a child might respond to the stimulus of the question 'What are three sixes?' with the response, 'Eighteen,' if the connection between the stimulus and response has been made correctly in the first instance, and reinforced over time. It should be noted here, that making a correct 'response' does not necessarily imply understanding. My daughter, for example, could tell me that thirteen is the square root of one-hundred and sixty-nine when she was two years old – she did not understand its meaning. She had learned by a series of simple rewards, in this case the approval of a parent to make a particular response to a particular stimulus. Behaviourism is based on what is termed Stimulus–Response (SR).

Behaviourism, a Definition

Behaviourism is a theory of learning focusing on observable behaviours, and discounting any mental activity. Learning is defined simply as the acquisition of new behaviour.

Behaviourists call this method of learning 'conditioning'. Two different types of conditioning are described and demonstrated as viable explanations of the way in which animals and humans alike, can be 'taught' to do certain things. First there is classical conditioning. This involves the reinforcement of a natural reflex, or some other behaviour that occurs as a response to a particular stimulus. A well-known example of this type of conditioning is the early work of Ivan Pavlov, a Russian physiologist at the start of the 20th century, who conditioned dogs to salivate at the sound of a bell. He noticed that dogs salivated when they ate, or even saw food. In his initial experiments he sounded a bell at the time when food was presented to the dogs. The sound of the bell became, for the dogs, an indication that food was about to be presented and eventually the dogs would salivate at the sound of the bell irrespective of the presence of food. The dogs had been conditioned to respond to the sound of the bell by producing saliva. Their behaviour had been successfully modified.

We talk about conditioning and conditioned responses in a general way, for example feeling fear at the sound of the dentist's drill, or at the sight of a syringe in preparation for an injection, are both examples of conditioned responses.

Pavlov identified four main stages in the process of classical conditioning and what follows from the initial connection between stimulus and response: acquisition, extinction, generalisation and discrimination.

Acquisition

The *acquisition* phase is the initial learning of the conditioned response – for example, the dog salivating at the sound of the bell.

Extinction

Once learned, a conditioned response will not stay in place permanently. *Extinction* is used to describe the disappearance of the conditioned response brought about by repeatedly presenting the bell, for example, without then presenting food.

Generalisation

After a conditioned response to one stimulus has been learned, the person may also respond to similar stimuli without further training. For example, if a child is bitten by a dog, the child may fear not only that dog, but all other dogs.

Discrimination

Discrimination is the opposite of generalisation. An individual learns to produce a conditioned response to one stimulus but not to another similar stimulus. For example, a child may show a fear response to freely roaming dogs, but may show no fear when a dog is on a lead.

The second type of conditioning is 'operant conditioning'. Operant conditioning is the most important type of behaviourist learning. It is more flexible than classical conditioning, and therefore seen as more useful. It involves reinforcing a behaviour by rewarding it. It can also work in a negative way, when an undesirable behaviour can be discouraged, by following it with punishment. In some cases simply not offering an expected reward for a particular behaviour is a sufficient punishment.

For example, if a mother gives her child a chocolate bar every day that he tidies his bedroom, before long the child may spend some time each day tidying. In this example, the tidying behaviour increases because it is rewarded. This rewarding is known as reinforcement. It is likely that the tidying behaviour would decrease, or stop completely if the rewards were suspended.

Skinner, a psychologist working in America in the 1930s, is the most famous psychologist in the field of operant conditioning. Skinner studied the behaviour of rats and pigeons, and made generalisations of his discoveries to humans. He used a device now called a Skinner box. The Skinner box was a simple, empty box in which an animal could earn food by making simple responses, such as pressing a lever. A normal, almost random, action by the animal, such as pressing a lever in the box, would result in a reward, such as a food pellet. As the rewards continued for the repetition of the action, the animal 'learned' that in order to be fed it must press the lever.

Skinner maintained that rewards and punishments control the majority of human behaviours, and that the principles of operant conditioning can explain human learning.

The key aspects of operant conditioning are:

Reinforcement

This refers to any process that strengthens a particular behaviour, and makes it likely that the behaviour will happen again. There are two types of reinforcement: positive and negative.

Positive Reinforcement

Positive reinforcement is a powerful method for controlling the behaviour of both animals and people. For people, positive reinforcers include basic items such as food, drink, approval, or even something as apparently simple as attention. In the context of classrooms, praise, house-points or the freedom to choose an activity are all used in different contexts as rewards for desirable behaviour.

Negative Reinforcement

As its name suggests, this is a method of decreasing the likelihood of a behaviour by pairing it with an unpleasant 'follow-up'. There is controversy about whether punishment is an effective way of reducing or eliminating unwanted behaviours. Laboratory experiments have shown that punishment can be an effective method for reducing particular behaviour, but there are clear disadvantages, especially in classroom situations. When punished, anger or aggression may result, or there may be other negative emotional responses.

Shaping

The notion of shaping refers to a technique of reinforcement that is used to teach animals or humans behaviours that they have never performed before. When shaping, the trainer begins by reinforcing a simple response that the learner can easily perform. Gradually more and more complex responses are required for the same reward. For example, to teach a rat to press an overhead lever, the trainer can first reward any upward head movement, then an upward movement of at least three centimetres, then six, and so on, until the lever is reached. Shaping has been used to teach children with severe mental retardation to speak by first rewarding any sounds they make, and then gradually only rewarding sounds which approximate to the words which are being taught. Animal trainers use shaping to teach animals. In classrooms shaping can be used to teach progressively complex skills, and more obviously to ensure the desired behaviour from children at such times as the end of the day, lining up for assembly and so on. When a teacher says something like, 'Let's see which table is ready,' it would not be unusual in many classrooms to witness many, if not all, of the children sitting up straight with folded arms, having quickly put their books in a pile and their writing tools in their correct homes.

There is a place for learning in classrooms, which relies on the principles of behaviourism. However, since behaviourism gives little importance to mental activity, concept formation or understanding, there are difficult problems to overcome when setting out philosophies of teaching and learning which depend wholly upon behaviourist approaches. With reference to behaviourism and the advent of computer use in schools, Daniel Chandler considers that 'The microcomputer is a tool of awesome potency which is making it possible for educational practice to take a giant step backwards' (Chandler 1984). Chandler is suggesting that some of the outdated drill and practice-style learning situations, for example, learning by rote, which often ignores understanding, might experience a rebirth through the work of the educational software designers who, perhaps, know little about more enlightened approaches to learning. Chandler was wary about the prospect of leaning without understanding. By far the most straightforward type of software to produce, at the time, and that requiring least use of creative educational and pedagogic thought, was the drill and practice type of programs in the early days of what became known as 'educational computing'.

Constructivist Theories

The area of constructivism, in the field of learning, comes under the broad heading of cognitive science. Cognitive science is an expansive area, and has its roots in the first half of the last century at a time when academics from the disciplines of psychology, artificial intelligence, philosophy, linguistics, neuroscience and anthropology, realised that they were all trying to solve problems concerning the mind and the brain.

Cognitive Science, a Definition

Cognitive scientists study, among other things, how people learn, remember and interact, often with a strong emphasis on mental processes and often with an emphasis on modern technologies. 'The study of intelligence and intelligent systems, with particular reference to intelligent behaviour' (Posner 1984).

Cognitive Psychology, a Definition

Cognitive psychology is the scientific study of mental processes such as learning, perceiving, remembering, using language, reasoning and solving problems.

Constructivism, a Definition

Constructivists view learning as the result of mental construction. Learning takes place when new information is built into and added onto what is already known. People learn best when they actively construct their own understanding.

Piaget

Jean Piaget is one of the best-known psychologists in the field of child development and learning. Many teachers are introduced to what is known as his 'developmental stage' theory, which sets out age-related developmental stages.

The stages begin with the sensori-motor stage and end with the stage of formal operations. The developmental stage theory is a useful guide to intellectual growth, but modern thought has gone beyond Piaget's view. Another aspect of Piaget's work is concerned with the growth of knowledge and understanding, and the ways in which new information is dealt with by young learners. Piaget's descriptions of assimilation and accommodation, which we will consider next, are not restricted to young learners, and give a good representation of the process of learning for learners of all ages.

For Piaget, learning is a process of adjustment to environmental influences. He describes two basic processes which form this process of adjustment. They are: *assimilation* and *accommodation*. Piaget's view is influenced by his background in biology, and he sees organisms, including human beings, as constantly seeking to maintain a stability in their existence. A physical example of this would be the maintenance of a constant body temperature. If external conditions change, get hotter for example, a sophisticated organism will make physical changes in order to maintain stability. The body's temperature regulation systems come into operation and a constant temperature is held. Piaget's model for learning is similar. External experiences can have an impact on what is already 'known'. It could be that a new experience can add to and reinforce a view that is held, or it could contradict a existing view. For example a young child might know that a small creature covered in fur, with four legs and a tail, is a dog. The more examples of dogs that the child comes across, the more secure this idea becomes. However, a cat is also small, furry and has a tail. New environmental experience – being introduced to a cat, contradicts the currently held view on the definition of a dog. The new information is added to the existing information, and gradually a deeper and broader understanding of creatures with fur is developed.

Assimilation: is the process whereby new knowledge is incorporated into existing mental structures. The knowledge bank is increased to include new information.
Accommodation: is the process whereby mental structures have to be altered in order to cope with the new experience which has contradicted the existing model.
Equilibration: is the process of arriving at a stable state where there is no longer a conflict between new and existing knowledge.

A young child is introduced to a large white object in a kitchen and it is explained, simply, that it is hot, and should not be touched. The word cooker is used and learned by the child. The child has an evolving mental structure which includes the images and ideas of a large white object, in a kitchen, the word 'cooker' and the idea that it should not be touched. Very soon after this experience the child may well walk towards the next large white object in the kitchen, actually a fridge, and call out the word 'cooker'. When corrected by the more knowledgeable adult, a problem arises. The mental model for large white objects in kitchens is incomplete, and new experience is creating a contradiction for the child. New information in the form of a simple explanation from a parent will add the new information to the existing model and learning will have taken place. The unstable has been made stable, and the child moves on to an encounter with a dishwasher.

Piaget's early work formed the basis of the constructivist movement. In constructivist learning theory, the key idea is that '. . . students actively construct their own knowledge: the mind of the student mediates input from the outside world to determine what the student will learn. Learning is active mental work, not passive reception of teaching' (Woolfolk 1993: 485).

In constructivist learning, individuals draw on their experience of the world around them, in many different forms, and work to make sense of what they perceive in order to build an understanding of what is around them.

Within constructivist theory there are, naturally, different interpretations of the basic ideas of the construction of knowledge and understanding. We will consider some of these interpretations, in particular the notion of mental frameworks which hold items of knowledge in a notional, complex structure, each item having numerous links to other related items, each link defined according to connections and interpretations constructed by the 'owner'. We will look at schema theory which gives a model of, and an explanation for, what underpins the complex process of building new knowledge and understanding.

Schema Theory

'Human beings understand the world by constructing models of it in their minds' (Johnson-Laird 1983).

Mental models, which have been described and examined by psychologists over many years (Piaget – 1920s onwards, Bartlett – 1930s, Schank – 1970s, Rumelhart

– 1980s, to mention but a few), and which are the basis of schema theory, are now fairly widely considered as a reasonable way of looking at learning, and as a description of the way that the process of learning unfolds. Johnson-Laird tells us that mental models are the basic structure of cognition: 'It is now plausible to suppose that mental models play a central and unifying role in representing objects, states of affairs, sequences of events, the way the world is, and the social and psychological actions of daily life' (Johnson-Laird 1983), and we are told by Holland that '. . . mental models are the basis for all reasoning processes' (Holland *et al.* 1986).

To look more closely at the idea of a schema we can describe it as a theoretical multi-dimensional warehouse for, almost innumerable, items of knowledge, a framework with numerous nodes and even more numerous connections between nodes. At each node there is a discrete piece of information or an idea. The piece of information can be in any one of a range of different forms – image, sound, smell, feeling and so on. Each node is connected to many others. The connections are made as a result of there being some sort of link between the connected items. The links are personal, and identical items in the theoretical warehouses of two different people could easily have very different links made for very different reasons. It is the adding of items to schemas and connecting them to other items that constitutes constructivist learning. There is no limit to the size to which a schema might grow. There is no limit to the number of connections within a schema that might be made, and there are no restrictions on how schemas might link and interconnect with other schemas. The more connections there are within and between schemas, the more construction has taken place and it is considered that knowledge and understanding have been gained.

Figure 2.1 (based on Davis 1991) is an attempt to represent a schema, though it must be understood that to draw a schema is essentially impossible.

Some of the characteristics of schemas (mental models, scripts) are:

- they are based on our general world knowledge and experiences;
- they are generalised knowledge about situations, objects, events, feelings and actions;
- they are incomplete and constantly evolving;
- they are personal;
- they are not usually totally accurate representations of a phenomenon;
- they typically contain inaccuracies and contradictions;
- they provide simplified explanations of complex phenomena;
- they contain uncertainty but are used even if incorrect;
- they guide our understanding of new information by providing explanations of what is happening, what it means and what is likely to result.

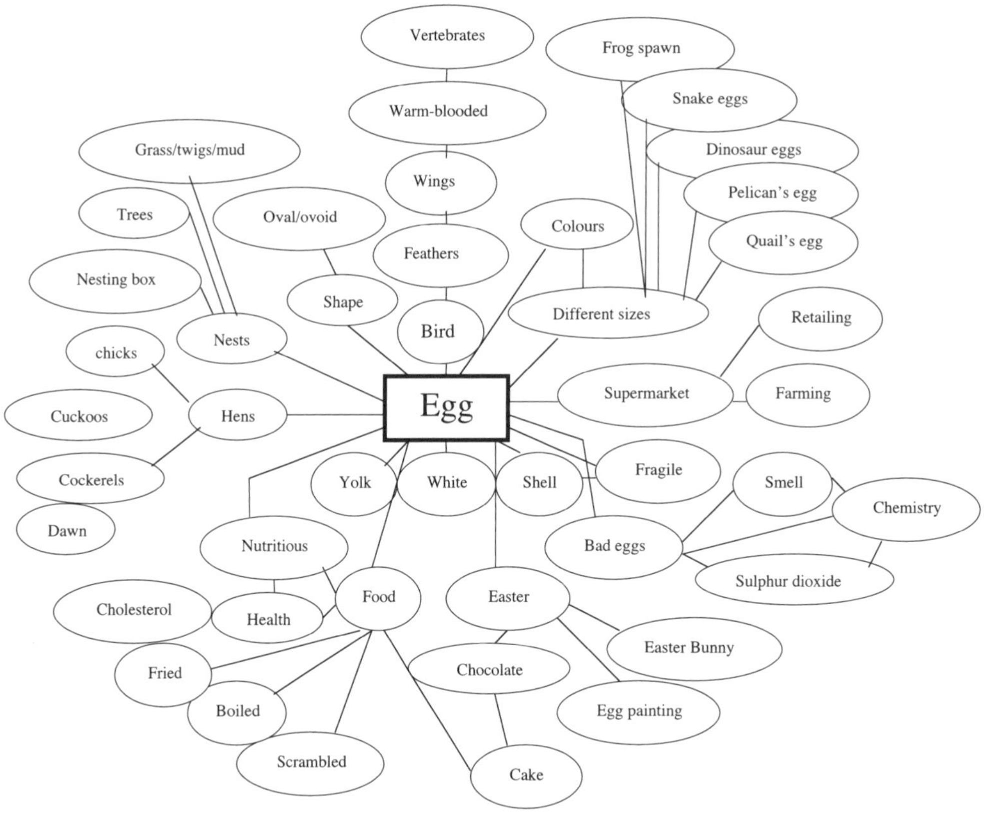
Egg
Vertebrates
Warm-blooded
Wings
Feathers
Bird
Frog spawn
Snake eggs
Dinosaur eggs
Pelican's egg
Quail's egg
Colours
Different sizes
Grass/twigs/mud
Trees
Oval/ovoid
Nesting box
Shape
Nests
chicks
Hens
Cuckoos
Cockerels
Dawn
Retailing
Supermarket
Farming
Yolk
White
Shell
Fragile
Smell
Chemistry
Bad eggs
Sulphur dioxide
Nutritious
Food
Easter
Cholesterol
Health
Easter Bunny
Chocolate
Fried
Boiled
Egg painting
Scrambled
Cake

Figure 2.1 *An attempt to represent a schema*

Prior knowledge has a crucial part to play in constructivist learning. An existing schema is the sum of an individual's current state of knowledge and understanding of a particular topic, event, action and so on. New learning concerned with the particular topic will involve the processes of accommodation and assimilation and the expansion, and increase in complexity, of the schema. For this reason it is very important that a schema which is to be the focus of these processes in the introduction of a new area of work in school, is activated. In simple terms, if new learning is to take place it is a very good idea to review what is already known about the topic in question. The starting point of what is already known and understood is very important if any new learning is to be effective. Schema activation is a process which can be encouraged in classroom situations, and teachers frequently make use of this idea in their work.

Schema Theory: Summary

Cognitive psychologists refer to units of knowledge as schemas, as a way of referring to conceptual knowledge which is stored in long-term memory. It is estimated that any adult would have hundreds of thousands of schemas in their memory, which would be interrelated in an almost infinite number of ways. New schemas are created and existing ones are constantly updated. This takes place every time that we read, listen to, or observe, or sense in any other way, anything new. New schemas are created every time that one fact is linked to another by a logical or semantic connection. Each schema is a sub-schema of another larger and related schema, and each schema has set of sub-schemas of its own.

Mayer (1983) gives four elements which describe a schema:

- general: a schema may be used in a wide variety of situations as a framework for understanding incoming information;
- knowledge: a schema exists in memory as something which a person knows;
- structure: a schema is organised around some theme;
- comprehension: a schema contains slots which are filled in by specific information.

Social Constructivism

The origins of the constructivist view of learning have their roots in the work of Piaget. Piaget's view of the growing child was what he called a 'lone scientist'. This description gives an image of a child alone, exploring the immediate environment and drawing conclusions about the nature and structure of the world. Social constructivism adds an important new dimension to the theory. Stress is laid upon interaction between the learner and others. The others can come in many forms but it is the dimension of social interaction that is crucial to the social constructivists. The main proponents of this branch of constructivism are Vygotsky, a Russian whose work was carried out towards the start of the 20th century but not available in the west until many years later, and Bruner, an American publishing his work in the second half of the 20th century.

Social constructivism gives a high priority to language in the process of intellectual development. Dialogue becomes the vehicle by which ideas are considered, shared and developed. The dialogue is often with a more knowledgeable other, but this need not always be the case. Dialogue with peers can be of equal value. Prior knowledge, naturally, has a part to play. It is an individual's prior and current knowledge that forms the basis of any contribution to a dialogue and it is with reference to existing knowledge and understanding (schemas) that new ideas and understanding can be constructed in the course of dialogue. When we consider the more knowledgeable other, it is easy to assume that this person will be a teacher, or a parent, but this need not be the case. More knowledgeable need not imply older, or a position of responsibility for learning. It is very often the case that learning will take place in very different environments. Most learning does not take place in school. Any social interaction with anybody at all may well lead to learning. The building and exchange which takes place in the course of a discussion, in any context at all, is likely for at least one of the participants, and often for both or all of them, to lead to a greater understanding of the topic of the conversation.

The role of the more knowledgeable other in formal learning situations is usually taken by a teacher. The teacher has the role of stimulating dialogue and maintaining its momentum. In a very real way, the teacher engages groups and individuals in dialogue and supports the development of understanding. The undertaking of this role, in a planned way, has a particular name and is known as scaffolding. To fully understand the concept of scaffolding we need to first look at another aspect of Vygotsky's work, which is the notion of a zone of proximal development.

The zone of proximal development is a refreshingly simple description of something which many teachers and other adults understand and work with. It is an idea from learning and developmental theory, which has impacted on practice over the last twenty years or so as more importance has been given to the notion of differentiation in teaching.

The zone of proximal development is a theoretical space of understanding that is just above the level of understanding of a individual given. It is the area of understanding that a learner will move into next. In the zone of proximal development a learner is able to work effectively, but only with support. The zone is necessarily different for each individual child. The process of learning involves moving into and across the zone and looking forward to the next stage, which will involve a similar journey. Sewell (1990) explains it as 'a point at which a child has partly mastered a skill but can act more effectively with the assistance of a more skilled adult or peer.'

Passing through the zone of proximal development is a process which can be aided by the intervention of another. A teacher can fulfil this role, and so can a range of other people. In planning work for children a teacher needs to take into account the current state of the understanding of the children in question. It has been suggested that a computer-based teaching situation can act as the more knowledgeable other in some well-designed situations (Sewell 1990).

Scaffolding is the process of giving support to learners at the appropriate time and at the appropriate level of sophistication to meet the needs of the individual. Scaffolding can be presented in many ways: through discussion – a good socially constructive approach; through the provision of materials; perhaps supplying practical apparatus to help in the solution of simple problems in arithmetic; or by designing tasks which match and give help appropriate to the individual; a list of words given to help in the process of completing an exercise designed to assist understanding; or a list of reminders concerning the process of undertaking the task in question.

Working collaboratively, in pairs or small groups, is an obvious socially constructive approach to learning. The converse of this would be working in a silent classroom, where contact with others is discouraged. There are times when quiet individual working is useful and important, and teachers are able to describe many times when a child should be encouraged and required to work alone and quietly. As a mainstay approach to teaching and learning, this would totally ignore all that we know about socially constructed knowledge and understanding.

Features of Constructivism

Constructivist learning theory is built around a set of important features which can be summed up as follows (after Jonassen *et al.* 1999):

- Knowledge construction and not knowledge reproduction is paramount.

The process is central to the learner's construction of new knowledge and understanding. It is the processes which the learner puts into place and uses which are important, rather than the fact of knowing something as an end product. A learner is actively engaged, and in control of the learning process. We will return to this important idea later.

- Learning can lead to multiple representations of reality.

When learning involves the use of a variety of resources (e.g. first-hand experience, secondary sources, interactive materials, independent research, dialogue) alternative viewpoints of the subject in question are formed; this in turn can be used to foster the critical thinking skills.

- Authentic tasks in a meaningful context are encouraged.

Authentic tasks, such as problem-solving, are used to situate learning in familiar and realistic contexts.

- Reflection on prior experience is encouraged.

Learners are prompted to relate new knowledge and concepts to pre-existing knowledge and experience which allows the 'new' to integrate with what is known already, adding to a learner's framework of understanding (schema) or amending it.

- Collaborative work for learning is encouraged.

Dialogue with others allows additional and alternate perspectives to be taken into account when developing personal conclusions. Different knowledge, points of view and understanding can be given and considered before moving on.

- Autonomy in learning is encouraged.

Learners are given, and accept increasing amounts of responsibility for their own learning. This happens in a number of different ways: by collaborating with others, working on self-generated problems, and the forming and testing of hypotheses, for example.

Situated Learning and Authentic Activity

Situated learning refers to the fact that all learning takes place in a context. The context may, or may not be familiar to the learner. If the context is unfamiliar to the learner, the learning will not necessarily proceed smoothly.

Situated learning (Lave and Wenger 1991) in part suggests that skills, knowledge and understanding which are learned, and even mastered, in one context may not necessarily be transferred successfully to another. Another aspect of situated learning which is more relevant here, is the notion that learning can be situated in social and cultural settings, and that if a learning activity falls beyond the cultural understanding of the learner, then learning is likely, at best, to be less successful than if had it been situated in a more familiar setting. For example, giving young children the task of investigating the pros and cons of fox hunting is very unlikely, without exceptionally detailed and sympathetic introductions and the provision of first-hand experience, to lead to good quality learning experiences if their cultural setting is a deprived inner-city area where there is little contact with the countryside and domestic or wild animals, and the emotions associated with the discovery of ravaged lambs or roosting hens are alien to them. In order to introduce the children to the ideas of making a case, and arguing for particular points of view, it would be far more reasonable to invite them to consider something within their cultural domain. The same would almost certainly be true in reverse; children brought up in a rural environment with little experience of city life might well find it difficult to understand, and learn from, notions concerning overcrowded housing estates and parents fearful of letting their children play and roam freely.

There is a link between the idea of learning being situated, and the need for authentic learning tasks. Much has been written on this matter (see for example, McFarlane 1997). Authentic tasks are . . . 'tasks which pupils can relate to their own experience inside and outside of school; tasks which an experienced practitioner would undertake' (Selinger 2001). When learning is made up of authentic tasks, there is a greater probability of engagement with the task and also with the information and ideas involved with the task. Authentic tasks are likely to hold the attention and interest of the children and lead to a deeper level of engagement than with another similar but 'non-authentic' or at least, less authentic, task. This links closely with the ideas put forward by the socio-cultural learning theorists. Bruner (1996), Brown Collins and Duigud (1989) and others support the need for culturally linked and authentic learning tasks. This has the desirable effect of making the difference between school learning and 'out of school learning' less well defined.

Metacognition

A short consideration of metacognition is appropriate here. Metacognition refers to the idea of an individual considering, being aware of and understanding their own mental and learning process. This awareness will have a bearing on an individual's recognition of their own learning and the ways in which they might learn best.

Metacognition, a Definition

Metacognitive knowledge is the knowledge that an individual has about their own cognition, and which can be used to consider and to control their cognitive processes. To work metacognitively is to consider, and take active control of the processes involved in learning and thinking as they are happening.

The term 'metacognition' is most closely associated with the psychologist John Flavell (1976, 1977). He tells us that metacognition consists of metacognitive knowledge and metacognitive experiences or regulation. Metacognitive knowledge is knowledge about cognitive processes, which an individual has come to understand, and can be used to control mental processes. 'Metacognition refers to one's knowledge concerning one's cognitive processes and products or anything related to them . . . metacognition refers, among other things, to the active monitoring . . . regulation and orchestration of these processes' (Flavell 1976). Brown (1987) offers a simpler version of this when he says that 'Metacognition refers loosely to one's knowledge and control of [one's] own cognitive system.'

When we are metacognitively aware, we are able to consider the ways and means of our own learning. These ways and means are usually very personal and at times idiosyncratic. Many of us have particular ways of learning for tests and exams, and we know that they are effective for us. In some respects this has connections with Gardner's multiple intelligence theory (Gardner 1993), which proposes the idea that we all have various levels of intelligence across a range of intellectual areas. There are also links with learning style, which can affect approaches which an individual favours and makes use of in learning situations. We actually learn in different ways to each other and we often choose to use our preferred learning style. If a particular approach to learning is encouraged by a teacher, it can lead to a situation where some pupils might well work and learn less effectively than others in the class.

Gardner's theory of multiple intelligences comes in part out of a concern that when intelligence is measured, the most commonly used devices (standard verbal and non-verbal reasoning tests) often don't allow those tested to demonstrate what they are really good at, or where their intelligence lies. Gardner gives us a set of different *intelligences* which as individuals we display more or less of, according to our particular intellectual make-up. There are eight of these intelligences:

- linguistic: enjoyment of and facility with reading, poetry and all things linguistic;
- logical/mathematical: enjoyment of and facility with maths and science, games of strategy and any logic-based pursuits;
- musical: enjoyment of and facility with music, listening, playing and perhaps composing;
- spatial/visual: enjoyment of and facility with images, drawing, construction games and tactile puzzles such as jigsaws;
- kinaesthetic: enjoyment of and facility with activities which involve touch and movement, dance, sport and other practical activities;
- interpersonal: enjoyment of and facility with other people, communication, leadership and the ability to empathise;
- intrapersonal: enjoyment of and facility with self-motivation, no dependence on others, awareness of one's own feelings more than those of others; often seen as shyness;
- naturalistic: enjoyment of and facility with the natural world, ability in recognising patterns and classification.

An individual's particular strengths and preferences in intelligences has a direct bearing upon the way in which learning takes place. Some with interpersonal strengths would be most likely to learn effectively in a social situation where relating ideas and knowledge to others can be encouraged. The opposite might be true for an individual with low interpersonal intelligence and a strength in intrapersonal intelligence.

To be aware of multiple intelligence strengths and our preferred or most effective learning approach is to be thinking metacognitively.

Deep and Surface Learning

Biggs and Moore (1993) outline the distinction between deep and surface learning (see Table 2.1). Deep learning, they suggest, is most likely to take place when the learner becomes very involved in the task(s) in question – they use the term 'engage' to illustrate their point. Surface learning comes about when the learner undertakes the minimum amount of work, or engagement (we will consider engagement later), that is possible. They continue by saying that: 'The deep approach is ideally what school learning should involves' (ibid, p.313). Biggs and Moore characterise three learner styles, or attitudes as a way of explaining the difference between deep and surface learning, and include a third category – the 'achieving' learner.

Table 2.1 Deep, surface and achieving learners

Deep Learner	Surface Learner	Achieving Learner
'I want to learn'	'I want to have fun'	'I want top marks'
Real involvement with the topic	Minimal amount of work	Cost-effective use of time
In-depth engagement with topic	Scratch the surface of the topic	Keen to make best use of time

A deep learner asked to read and consider the plot and implications of a play or story, would do just that. Not only would they know the story in detail, but they would be able to take the perspective of different characters, consider the ramifications of certain aspects of the story and be able to relate the story to a wider perspective. A surface learner when confronted with the same task would be able to relate the story, and name the characters and perhaps little more. An achieving learner would be interested in being able to answer questions in an exam, or being able to impress the teacher with their knowledge. Understanding, to an achieving learner, is a secondary consideration.

It is not difficult to identify the three types of learner. In order to stay out of trouble, with teachers, or perhaps parents, many children might take the surface approach, especially when the subject matter is of little interest and there is no intrinsic motivation to engage more deeply.

This raises questions about motivation to learn, and the difference between intrinsic and extrinsic motivation. It is a behaviouristic approach to teaching that imposes motivation from the outside. Possibilities of rewards, and the possibility of sanctions can be strong motivators. However a far more lasting and productive motivation comes from within. As we have seen in the section dealing with the situatedness of learning and the importance of the cultural setting of learning and the use of authentic tasks, there are ways of increasing interest in learning activities and possibly generating intrinsic motivation. It is worth considering briefly the results of increased motivation to learn, as it forms an important part of the role of teachers. Without motivation of any type, there is a very limited chance that learning of any sort will take place. This is what makes an understanding of motivation so important. Throughout this book, the emphasis is on achieving learning objectives, and in order to achieve those objectives effectively, there needs to be a selection of strategies, underpinned by theoretical perspectives, which create interest in the topic in question and a motivation to learn more about it.

Raised levels of motivation have been shown to lead to improvements in four areas of classroom life:

- increased commitment to learning;
- enhanced sense of achievement;
- increased self-esteem;
- improved behaviour.

Examples in research findings of improvements in the four areas above are taken from technology-centred work, since the main thrust of this book is the use of technology, and in particular the Internet, to enhance learning. Rockman, and separately, Becker, have reported that teachers providing more technology-centred lessons have seen that their pupils are motivated to continue using computers at times other than their formal lesson time. This will not be a surprise to many teachers who find it difficult to call an end to some computer-based work (Becker 2000; Rockman 2000). Pupils involved in Challenge 2000, an internet-based teaching and learning resource, were noticeably keen to work in their own time, both before and after school, as well as during lessons. There were no problems with keeping pupils on task, with high levels of involvement and enthusiasm (Harris and Kington 2002). Heightened interest, engagement and improved behaviour were noted in a case study based in a real environment close to the school in question, making use of new and largely very well-received computer technology (Pritchard 1997).

Making good use of ICT can lead to an enhanced sense of achievement for many pupils who have not previously considered themselves to be good at school work. Learning improvements and heightened motivation have been found in literacy and numeracy (Moseley and Higgins 1999), geography and English (Hennessy 2000; Van Daal and Reitsma 2000) and for pupils with special needs who have produced work of a higher than expected standard (Harris and Kington 2002). As with any work whether it relies on ICT or not, if it is either too difficult or too easy it can serve as a serious de-motivator (Cox 1997). This relates directly to the notion, from Vygotsky's work, of the zone of proximal development.

Engagement

Everything about the constructivist approach to learning, in a simple and practical way, points towards the importance of learners getting as close to the content of what they hope to learn as possible. As we will see, this is possible in a wide range of different ways. This closeness to the material can be termed 'engagement'.

For children to understand new information, they must become actively involved with it. There is a five-stage model which puts engagement at the start of the process of learning, put forward by a group of Australian teachers and academics, which takes a wholly constructivist approach, and within which the importance of the individual and of activity is stressed. As we know, learning is not a passive process, and so, with reference to what is known about effective learning, and with due attention paid to the notion of engagement, it is possible to map out approaches to learning with Internet resources that encompass the best and most effective of what is known. The five-stage model (Reid *et al.* 1989) of engagement – exploration – transformation – presentation – reflection sets out a route to be followed with work of this nature.

They describe engagement as 'the time during which students acquire information and engage in an experience that provides the basis for, or content of, their ensuing learning . . .' (ibid, p.28). The next stage in the model – exploration – is closely related to the stage of engagement. This stage can be an open-ended process, where children follow their instincts, but possibly a more profitable approach for teachers to take with their classes is to set short tasks which develop both engagement and exploration. These tasks are designed to give the child an overview of what is contained in the information under consideration and may take many forms, as we will see later.

Transformation is the stage in which information with which the child has engaged, and has explored, might be re-configured into a form which allows for presentation (the next stage), but importantly, transformed into a format which will, from the teacher's point of view, enable learning objectives to be met. From the point of view of the child, certain questions will now be able to be answered. Transformation and the resultant presentation is not the end of the process. Time to reflect upon what has been undertaken, the process and the content, gives the opportunity for internalisation, and for a deeper level of understanding to be developed. Reflection can also take many forms. One common approach is to ask children to give a short presentation/explanation of what they have been doing and what they have learned. This can take a variety of different formats, prepared for a variety of different audiences – a poster to display, a newspaper front page, a multimedia presentation and so on. Sometimes teachers feel that some form of assessment is necessary, and the opportunity to revise before a test could be viewed as the stage of reflection.

Selinger (2001) tells us that she found 'Much Internet activity consists of unstructured searches, ill-defined tasks, and children's work which consists of text and images cut and pasted into a report. Questioning children about their reports in these situations often reveals no evidence of understanding or learning.' Her research, and the work of others, (including Pritchard and Cartwright 2003) show up the poor quality of some Internet-based work.

Poor preparation when using the Internet, or indeed any other sizeable resource can lead to a lack of purpose and to very little discernible learning. Purpose, or focus, seems to be a very important element of being successful when working with large information sources. We will see later that there are strategies which teachers can develop for children to use which can give a focus and a well-defined purpose to this sort of work.

Bereiter and Scardamalia (1987) describe a model of the writing process which they term 'knowledge transformation'. Knowledge transformation can be seen as information, possibly from a number of different sources, being reconstructed in order to answer certain questions and to help meet particular learning objectives. This model is characterised by the writer alone accomplishing what is normally accomplished through the medium of social dialogue. Knowledge is considered and 'worked upon' by the individual and engagement takes place. This dialogue, which forms an important element of the thinking underpinning social constructivism, is seen as the medium through which learning takes place. A child working alone cannot take part in an actual dialogue, which has the possibility of allowing engagement with the knowledge and ideas of the topic in question, but by undertaking a process of knowledge transformation, a similar process may come into play, and effective learning may be possible.

Encouraging Engagement

We have seen that without engagement with the content of an activity, effective learning is far less likely to be the result of anything which teachers ask children to do. It can be surmised that an important element of the role of the teacher is to encourage engagement, since without some measure of involvement with information and ideas, and the undertaking of activity centred on the content, (Bereiter and Scardamalia's knowledge transformation), there is a greatly reduced opportunity for effective learning to take place, especially the deep learning which is the aim of most teaching situations.

There are many effective ways of encouraging children to engage with their work. Taking into account the prior knowledge of the children, the level of difficulty, the social and cultural context, and the general level of interest of the subject matter, will all help with the need for engagement. In each of the succeeding chapters specific approaches related to the type of Internet resource in question will be considered.

When making use of the Internet to access information, if no guidance is given, and if clear and focused tasks are not set, there is a distinct possibility that the quality of the work carried out will be very poor (Pritchard and Cartwright 2004). Very little engagement with ideas will take place and there is likely to be wholesale copying – by the modern method of course, that is, cutting and pasting. When children are encouraged to make use of massive information sources, with little or no help, plagiarism will be the order of the day for many, and for the others the likelihood is that very little meaningful or lasting learning will take place (Lewis, Wray and Rospigliosi 1995). Good habits which will discourage copying and plagiarism can be encouraged from an early stage. We will see later how particular approaches to information reliant work can be structured in ways which do not encourage direct, cut and paste, copying. This is very important.

Exactly the same 'rules' apply for the planning of lessons which incorporate the use of the Internet as would apply in almost any other situation.

Lessons:

- need a clear focus and goals, with explicit learning objectives;
- need to be based upon the pupils' existing knowledge;
- need to be set in an appropriate context;

and

- there needs to be scope for social interaction and for activity;
- the lesson needs to be planned in such a way that it aims to move the pupils' learning forward.

The points above can all be traced back to what is known about the way that we learn, and to the work of many psychologists and educationalists in the field of learning. It would be unrealistic to suggest that if all of the above were in place then effective learning is certain to result, since, as all teachers know, there are a great many variables, some of which are controllable, and others which are not, but can so easily influence the outcome of any particular lesson. However, taking into account what is known about learning and how children learn will increase the possibility of effective learning resulting from the activity undertaken. Wray and Lewis (1997) single out four aspects of learning theory which they consider to be of paramount importance:

- learning is a process of interaction between what is known and what is to be learned;
- learning is a social process;
- learning is a situated process;
- learning is a metacognitive process.

From these four aspects of theory they go on to formulate four principles for teaching. These four principles, which are very close in nature to the 'rules' proposed above, can be seen as universal, and not simply applying in text-based or information-rich settings:

- learners need enough previous knowledge and understanding to enable them to learn new things; they need help making links with new and previous knowledge explicit;
- provision should be made for social interaction and discussion in groups of varying sizes, both with and without the teacher.

- meaningful contexts for learning are very important; it must be remembered that what is meaningful for a teacher is not necessarily meaningful for the child.
- children's awareness of their own thought processes should be promoted.

CHAPTER 3

Using words and word activities from the Internet

Amongst the innumerable locations which make up the Internet are hundreds of thousands of sites which include excellent teaching resources. Some are not designed as such and are there for other reasons. They can, nonetheless, be very useful in classroom learning situations. The very nature of the Internet means that it is endowed with some of the features which can go towards creating a context for effective learning: it is motivating, in many cases it is culturally and socially appropriate, it can lead to authentic tasks using 'real' up-to-date and relevant information and it often stimulates discussion. If, added to these features it can be shown that work involving the Internet is based on well-established prior knowledge, that new information, of any sort, is assimilated into current forms of knowledge, and that the necessary engagement with task and information alike gives the opportunity of deep learning to take place, the Internet becomes an even more powerful learning resource.

In this chapter we will look at some of the ways in which children can be encouraged to engage in tasks which make use of and rely upon words, in different formats, and in different subject areas, from the Internet.

The phrase 'use of words' may well bring to mind 'English' and 'Literacy', and there is vast scope for work in these areas, but the scope extends beyond the area of literacy and language development. We will consider activities using Internet resources in language and literacy related areas, but we will also spread further afield into other subject areas.

We will look at ways of encouraging engagement when working with factual information, which is in the main, presented in the form of words. The approaches that we will consider here are likely to be effective no matter what the source of the information: Internet, CD-ROM, books, posters, leaflets and so on. Encouraging engagement in other types of Internet work will be exemplified in later chapters.

A starting point, in all cases, for work with information, would be to encourage children to consider what it is that they already know or understand about the topic in question. The full extent to which this is done will depend upon particular circumstances. If, for example, the topic is completely new there may well be a need to 'dredge up' what is known to individuals and to the class as a whole; with a more familiar topic, or a topic which has been covered more recently, this need is less pronounced.

The activation of prior knowledge is given prime importance in the 'Extending Interactions with Text' (EXIT) model devised by Wray and Lewis (1997). This model is primarily concerned with texts, in their widest interpretation, and so it will be explored here. There are other models too, which we will consider before moving on.

The first stage of the ten-stage EXIT model (see Table 3.1) requires that children are encouraged to review the state of their existing knowledge and sometimes, understanding. It is termed the 'activation of prior knowledge'. It relates very closely to the constructivist notion that new knowledge and understanding is built upon a foundation of what exists already. By focusing attention on to existing knowledge the process of building new knowledge and understanding is given a head start.

Table 3.1 The EXIT model

Stages in the Process	Appropriate questions to ask
Activation of previous knowledge	What do I already know?
Establishing a purpose	What do I need to find out and what will I do with the information?
Locating information	Where and how will I get this information?
Adopting an appropriate strategy	How should I use this source of information to get what I need?
Interacting with the text	What can I do to make me understand this better?
Monitoring understanding	What can I do if there are parts I do not understand?
Making a record	What should I make a note of from this information?
Evaluating information	Which items of information should I believe and which should I keep an open mind about?
Assisting memory	How can I help myself remember the important parts?
Communicating information	How should I let other people know about this?

Another important principle of work with information is to encourage children to focus on a specific aspect of what is probably a wide field of interest. In the EXIT model this is covered under the 'Establishing a Purpose' heading. Without clear focus and a well-thought-out purpose, work using a large amount of information, such as the Internet can provide, is liable to become difficult to sustain and will not lead to an effective learning experience. Wray and Lewis (1997) describe the use of a KWL grid as a starting point for research work with non-fiction texts. This is a general approach, not restricted to use with information specifically from web-based or other electronic sources. Use of a KWL grid is likely to assist the process of activating prior knowledge, and, with support and practice, likely to help in the process of focusing the activity. KWL comes from: 'What do I KNOW – What do I WANT to find out – What have I LEARNED (KWL)'. The use of such a grid encourages children to focus on what they already know about a topic, to identify what they would like to know about it and then to plan and find something out and note what they have learned. The KWL grid (alternatively known as 'Prior Knowledge and Reaction') was first put forward by Ogle (1989) and has been further extended by Wray and Lewis (1997) (see Table 3.2 for an example KWL Grid).

Table 3.2 A KWL grid

KWL Grid

Topic:_______________ **Name:**_______________

What do I know already?	What do I want to find out?	What have I learned?

Another approach which could well be of value in work of this nature with children, is the use of a writing frame. This notion, also explained by Wray and Lewis (1997) is a simple scaffolding device which gives a structure for children to use when writing in a format or style which is new to them (see Figure 3.1, an example of a simple writing frame).

This report is to tell you something about . . .

There are three / four / five things that are very important / interesting / surprising about . . .

They are:

1.

2.

3.

These facts came from . . .

The reasons why they are important / interesting / surprising are . . .

Figure 3.1 *Example of a writing frame for non-fiction writing*

Other Models and Approaches

These systems of approaching non-fiction text encourage the asking of questions, the making of notes and other activities which encourage all important cognitive activity and engagement. Of the models which follow, some are on a larger scale than others. Of the simple models it could be said that they are simply strategies or approaches that have the potential to assist in the wider process of building understanding from written sources. This is possibly true, but it does not undermine their usefulness in classroom contexts, and for that reason they are included here with the slightly more grandiose information handling models.

Earlier models, which in some cases are little more than lists designed to assist teachers in the planning of information-dependent work, set out stages which the work with information should progress through. Winkworth (1977) put forward the following:

(1) define the subject and purpose of the enquiry;

(2) locate the information;

(3) select appropriate information;

(4) organise the information;

(5) evaluate the information;

(6) communicate your results.

Michael Marland (Marland 1981), developed a system which has been influential over the years in the development of teaching about how to deal with sources of information. He also set out stages of activity which children should work through, this time formulated as questions:

(1) What do I need to do?

(2) Where could I go?

(3) How do I get the information?

(4) Which resources should I use?

(5) What should I make a record of?

(6) Have I got the information that I need?

(7) How should I present it?

(8) What have I achieved?

Marland's stages include the final evaluative and reflective aspect which is missing in other models.

Tann (1988) has a similar set of stages:

(1) identifying information that is wanted;

(2) selecting possible sources of information;

(3) locating information;

(4) extracting and recording information;

(5) interpreting/integrating/interrogating information;

(6) presenting findings.

The models above have been criticised for ignoring what is known as the transactional aspect of reading. This refers to interaction between reader and the text. Transactional reading involves a series of predictions made by the reader who, in doing so, is considering far more about the content of the text than the decoding of the individual letters, words and sentences. Goodman (1967) described this interpretation of the reading process as 'a concept-driven guessing game'. In transactional reading, readers are sampling the text and trying to confirm predictions which they make as their reading progresses. This is very much in the way of engaging at more than a superficial level with the content of what is being read. The EXIT model, and those considered below, take the interaction between text and reader more seriously. The EXIT model includes an explicit reference to the idea of interacting, as a way of leading towards a more metacognitive approach.

Before we look at some of the other models, or strategic approaches to work with information, we will briefly examine a way in which teachers can encourage their children to read in a more transactional way, which is a very good sharing experience for whole groups and their teacher. This is 'meta-reading'. Meta-reading is not, as the title might suggest, reading about reading, but reading at the same time as expressing thoughts, making predictions and asking questions about what is being read. It is a way of reading which many of us use instinctively in certain situations. For example a teacher reading to a group of children will stop from time to time and talk to the group. The reason for stopping might be to ascertain that particular words are understood, or other 'low' level reasons, but on other occasions the reasons for stopping are more to do with a higher level of interaction with the text. When reading for information, there is a strong case for practising meta-reading. There is also a place for it in the reading of fiction. In meta-reading four actions take place:

- predicting;
- clarifying;
- questioning;
- summarising (Lewis and Wray 1997).

When a teacher reads to a group and models this style of reading, children begin to learn about interacting with the text and going beyond simply 'saying the words' to themselves. The short passages below give examples of teachers who are reading in this way to groups of children. The breaks from the text are spaces where the teacher is able to give a commentary, ask questions, sometimes rhetorically, make predictions and encourage the children to do the same. In the extract, the words from the text are in normal type, and the teacher's words are in italic. To encourage meta-reading is to prepare children for the task of dealing with texts which can supply a lot of information if they are approached in a way that allows the information to be accessed, rather than in a way that simply allows individual words and phrases to be decoded and forgotten. Obviously, children who have difficulty with reading still need to be catered for. Texts should, naturally, be at the correct level of difficulty, and appropriate support should be available wherever possible.

Example One

The first people of Britain lived among its forests and hills. They hunted, fished and gathered wild plants. About 4000 BC, people with stone axes began clearing the forests to grow crops and graze cattle. *It says that they started clearing the forests about 4000 years BC, Before Christ that is, but it doesn't say when the first people lived in Britain. We'll have to find out about that.* By 2500 BC, Britons used copper and bronze tools. They turned the forests into farms, fields, woods and pasture. *It doesn't say what sort of crops does it? Any ideas? Maybe we should try to find out about that too.*

Stone-using farmers made their tools with flint. They buried their dead in huge tombs of earth or rocks. The bronze-users dug round burial mounds called barrows. They also built Stonehenge and other stone circles. *So, what was Stonehenge exactly, and why did they build stone circles?*

Iron tools were made by people called Celts, whose homeland was in central Europe. By about 500 BC, the Celts had moved westward and into Britain. *Does anyone know about the Celtic areas of Britain now? We can find out where these people eventually settled and what became of them I think.* They lived in tribes, or large groups, which often fought each other for the lands they settled.

In a Celtic village homes were mostly round, with thatched roofs, the walls were made of stone, or wattle (woven branches) and daub (clay or mud cement). A wooden fence was put up between the homes and land beyond. Ox-wagons carried supplies from the fields *We know what an ox is, don't we?* and farm animals were kept in enclosures for safety. Craftsmen made tools, horseshoes and pots; the other villagers made huts, threshed corn, ground grain and brewed beer. *The horseshoes were probably made of iron, I think. We could find out when different metals were used and make a metal time line perhaps.*

Example 2

On the night of November 4th, *not the 5th then,* in the year of 1605 Guy Fawkes waited in the rented house next to the Houses of Parliament. *We knew about the rented house, didn't we?* Later he went secretly in to the cellars next door, through the tunnel which he and the other conspirators had prepared. *Yes, and the tunnel.* He was to light the fuse to the gunpowder and blow up the King and all of Parliament. This was not to be however, because of the warning given by Monteagle, soldiers were waiting for him. *We don't know who Monteagle was, do we? We ought to find out about him, if it was a 'he'.* He, *Guy Fawkes,* was caught and the gunpowder was discovered.

Guy Fawkes and the others who had plotted with him were executed. *They were executed . . . killed, in a very unpleasant way I think. Some of you might want to find out about that.* The loyal citizens of England celebrated this event by lighting bonfires and some made effigies of Guy Fawkes to burn on their fire. This practice has lasted many years and still today we celebrate in November with bonfires and fireworks.

Survey – Question – Read – Recite – Review (SQ3R)

SQ3R is a system of approaching texts which is designed to give the reader the greatest chance of coming to understand and retain what is being read. This aim is not different to the other systems and strategies in this area, the difference is in the implementation.

There are five stages in the SQ3R model: Survey, Question, Read, Recite, Review. (There is also a variant entitled SQ4R in which wRite is included, which is a useful addition.) Below is an outline of the SQ3R process.

1. **Survey** the passage before you read; look at:
   - the title, headings and sub-headings;
   - any captions under pictures, charts, graphs or maps;
   - the introductory and concluding paragraphs;
   - the summary, if there is one.

2. **Question** at the same time as surveying:
   - turn the title and sub-headings into questions;
   - read questions at the end of the chapters or after each sub-heading, for example, the title 'The Feudal System' can be altered into 'What is the Feudal System?';
   - ask, 'What have I been told about this passage?' by the teacher for example;
   - ask, 'What do I know already about this subject?'

3. **Read**, and:
   - look for answers to your questions;
   - answer questions at the beginning or end of sentences or paragraphs;
   - re-read captions under pictures, graphs, etc.;

- Take special note of all the underlined, italicised, bold printed words or phrases;
- read more slowly when you get to a difficult passage;
- re-read parts which are not clear.

4. **Recite** after you've read a section:

- take notes from the text but write the information in your own, simplified way;
- ask yourself questions aloud about what you have just read and/or summarise, in your own words, what you read;
- underline or highlight important points you read;
- use the method of reciting which best suits you, but remember, the more senses you use the more likely you are to remember what you read, – e.g. seeing, saying, hearing or, even better, seeing, saying, hearing, writing. It is in this section as well as the next, where the fourth 'R', referring to 'write' is sometimes inserted.

5. **Review.**

   This refers to looking back at what has been done, usually after a break. Some versions of SQ3R suggest a daily, and then weekly review, but in the primary school context this is not necessarily practical or desirable. Certainly re-visiting notes from a text, or looking back at the highlighted sections is a very useful action. When looked at in the context of revision for exams, some would say this is essential. As a part of the review process, the making of further notes, or of setting ideas out diagrammatically can be helpful.

Many competent readers make use of the type of approach set out here. They do it instinctively and in more or less detail according to their particular purpose. These actions of competent, accomplished readers form the basis of the different models being considered here.

The point about the use of senses is related to what is believed to be a Chinese proverb: What I see I forget; what I hear I remember; what I do I understand. This has wider ramifications for the educational process of course and refers to more than reading, but the act of writing, based on reading, is indeed an action and leads to opportunities for greater engagement with the ideas in the text.

Preview: REad to understand – Process to learn (PREP). Mk I

This model, which is made up of three steps, is also used instinctively by many readers. Indeed, as we have seen, accomplished readers for information, do make use of many of the techniques discussed here, and others besides.

Step 1: Preview
Preparation to Read: questions before reading

At this stage the reader is encouraged to look through the text and, in a sense, see the lie of the land. Questions should be asked at this stage. For example:

- Does this look interesting?
- Is it suitable for me? (i.e. will I understand it?)
- Which section seems most promising?

Step 2: Read to Understand
While reading certain questions should be kept in mind, and certain techniques used for helping in the process and for help if the passage is re-read at a later stage. For example:

- underline or highlight certain words, sentences or short passages;
- write short marginal notes;

  (These are only suitable if the text is in a format where marking it is allowable i.e. not a library book. For this reason teachers sometimes provide copies of pages from books, or printed web pages.)
- keep a brief record of the most important points from the text in note form.

Step 3: Process to Learn
In this final stage, more activity is called for, leading to more engagement with the information and ideas in the text. Activities can include:

- writing a short summary;
- creating visual study tools – diagrammatic representation of the ideas and information;
- creating mnemonics or simple and memorable rhymes;
- reciting main points or notes taken.

This model does not include the idea of telling others, or exchanging thoughts about a text which has been read by more than one, but it would be a sound, socially constructive, approach to take.

PREP Mk II

There is another, related, process with the same acronym which can have benefits, and may well suit some readers better than other approaches. It is known as the Pre-Reading Plan (Holbrook 1984). In this system, the teacher plays an important role initially, by leading the proceedings and by modelling the activity. As a group, possibly the whole class, any prior knowledge of content of a piece of text is discussed and children are asked to look at and comment on the organisation of the text. While they are looking at the layout and organisation of the text, they should skim the text by reading the first and last sentence of each paragraph and the entire first and last paragraphs. Next, pupils should survey the text, looking at the pictures and diagrams, the titles and any bold or italic text to help generate predictions about the text. As a group, the children will work on PReP to call up prior knowledge that is relevant to the content area. In the course of discussion they will verbalise associations that come to mind concerning the concepts in the text which they have scanned. This brings the children's content schemas to the fore, which we have considered earlier and is known to be an important step in dealing with new information. The final step in this version of PReP is to look at the vocabulary related to the content. Children should look at the words that they are encountering, possibly for the first time, and discuss these as a class.

It is quite likely that one or another of the approaches to reading for information will suit different readers in different ways. Insisting on one way of learning, or reading for information, is not always a good policy, as each of us have preferences. This is related to different 'learning styles' (Kolb 1984, for example) and also to Gardner's theory of 'Multiple Intelligences' (Gardner 1983, 1993). A part of the role of the teacher is to allow children to arrive at the point where they are able, independently, to select an approach to their work which suits them best. This process can be accelerated if children are introduced to different approaches; of course, the danger is that they may become confused and end up with no real understanding of any particular approach. This must be guarded against.

Directed Activities Related to Texts (DARTs)

DARTs provide another setting within which engagement with the facts and ideas in non-fiction texts is encouraged. DARTs were first written about by Lunzer and Gardner (1979) and later by Davies and Greene (1984). The names cover a wide range of different types of activities all of which serve to focus the attention of the reader on the important elements of the text as a way of encouraging engagement and increasing the amount of cognitive activity which takes place.

DARTs are divided into two broad categories, namely, 'Reconstruction Activities' and 'Analysis Activities'. Reconstruction, or completion activities, are essentially problem-solving activities and make use of a modified version of the text in question. The text, or diagram, is reproduced by the teacher with parts missing: words, phrases or labels are deleted, or alternatively, the text is broken into segments which have to be re-ordered or re-arranged. The activities have game-like characteristics where the game involves hunting for clues in order to make full sense of the text. To complete these activities it is necessary to read and often re-read the text and to think about the sense and meaning of the information, often in some depth. *Analysis activities* do not need the text to be modified, it is used precisely as it is. These activities seem to be more educational in nature than the game-like reconstruction activities; the aim of the activities being to find a particular meaning or to seek for particular 'information targets' in the text. Searching for the targets involves children in locating and categorising the information in the text. This, in turn, leads to detailed engagement with the information and ideas in the text.

The Higher Order Information Handling Skills

The National Council for Educational Technology (NCET) produced a pack of resources for teachers which gives a model for information use, and also sound advice for making use of, and more importantly, making sense of information. *Making Sense of Information* (NCET 1995), a study pack and video, describes five types of higher-order information handling skills:

- *decision-making skills* – the ability to decide what data will serve the purpose of the enquiry and what sources are appropriate;
- *classifying skills* – the ability to adopt a variety of approaches to sorting, searching, organisation and presentation of data, to understand a range of classification systems and to seek out connections;
- *questioning skills* – the ability to ask pertinent questions that will probe the data and lead to meaningful answers;
- *analytical skills* – the ability to make inferences from the information in a reasoned and logical manner;
- *explanatory skills* – the ability to apply existing knowledge to draw conclusions about the nature and significance of what has been observed and to put forward a reasoned case to help explain new findings.

These skills, which can be common to many different information handling activities, are put into the form of a *process loop*.

Starting point: This is the point in an investigative activity where children have the skills which they need in order to allow them to begin work, and a context is set for them. They possibly have experience of searching for information, or they

Table 3.3 The NCET process loop

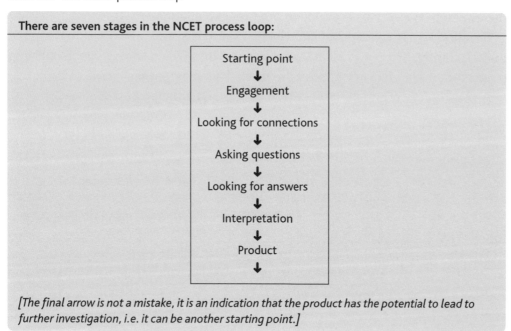

There are seven stages in the NCET process loop:
Starting point ↓ Engagement ↓ Looking for connections ↓ Asking questions ↓ Looking for answers ↓ Interpretation ↓ Product ↓
[The final arrow is not a mistake, it is an indication that the product has the potential to lead to further investigation, i.e. it can be another starting point.]

are at least in a position to pursue a search with the minimum of guidance. More likely, they will be directed towards either a particular site or set of sites, or particular CD-ROM. They also have a purpose for searching and considering information. The purpose may be ill-defined at this stage, for example, 'Let's find out more about the Tudors.' This purpose will be refined and become more focused at a later stage – asking questions.

Engagement: The purpose of the investigation is established and the children's interest has been stimulated. This stage of engagement is where information is gathered in a undiscriminating way, freely, and often according to children's particular interests.

Looking for connections: Information which has been gathered is sorted and classified. In terms of the earlier discussion in this chapter, this too is a part of the process of engagement with the information.

Asking questions: Children are encouraged to look at the information which they have gathered with *questioning* eyes. The organised information is likely to encourage children to raise questions about relationships, or anomalies. This is something which children are likely to need a good deal of help with, especially in the initial stages of this type of work.

Looking for answers: The information can be investigated in ways designed to establish the answers to questions posed by the children. This can include looking for further examples of the same relationship or looking for exceptions to rules.

Interpretation: This stage involves looking carefully, and in a discriminatory manner, at the findings. Possibly checking and confirming results. Instead of attempting to answer the question 'What?' the children are encouraged to answer the question 'Why?' This is a time to attempt explanations.

Product: Newly *constructed* knowledge now exists, and possibly a new level of understanding. This in itself may raise questions which may serve as starting points for another journey around the process loop, or perhaps parts of it.

An example of the loop in practice will illuminate the process (Table 3.4).

Table 3.4 The loop in practice

The Tudors: searching and using information sources:	
Stage One:	The topic is introduced and the context for the investigation is set. The children have some information searching skills – basic use of the Internet. The children are ready to proceed. Some *introductory* searching can be undertaken as a whole-class demonstration, this serves to reinforce the process.
Stage Two:	Children in small groups investigate a part of the breadth of information which is available. This may well be driven by an interest generated by having come across some facts about the topic from another source, or it may be less well focused.
Stage Three:	Snippets of information which have been collected can be sorted, and considered with a view to *finding out more* about a particular aspect of life in Tudor times.
Stage Four:	One particular topic is made the focus – food for example, and questions are formulated. 'What did they eat most of all?'; 'Did the rich people eat the same as the poor people?'
Stage Five	Answers to questions are sought. This need not be restricted to the use of computer-based sources of information.
Stage Six:	When more information has been gathered, searches completed, findings studied and so on, a considered view on the answers to questions can be attempted. 'No, they couldn't have eaten potatoes all of the time, because it says here that someone called Walter Raleigh was supposed to have found them in America and he didn't go there until 1578.'
Stage Seven:	*New* knowledge has been established through a process of questioning and investigation. This may lead to further questions of course – 'What did they eat then?'

This process is generic and can be applied in a range of different situations. The process is not newly invented for the purposes of the use of computer-based systems, but the ready availability of so much information, much of it mediated by the Internet, makes the application of this process to learning situations an important consideration for teachers. In the light of the theoretical descriptions of constructivist learning considered earlier, it can be seen to be a sound process likely to lead to learning.

Preparing to Work with the Internet

If children are to reap the optimum benefit from the content of websites, especially younger users, and especially in educational settings, it is more or less essential that both the children and the work are very well prepared, and subsequently well supported. Practising the skills which will be used in trial, or dry-run, situations can be very useful. The skills associated with the effective use of information – reading, skimming, extracting important points, note-taking, re-configuring ideas, presenting ideas for others, for example, can be introduced and worked through in small-scale versions of an actual research project. This is reminiscent, for some, of an element of the National Curriculum for Design and Technology (D&T). The idea of a focused practical task (fpt) was introduced in an early incarnation of the National Curriculum orders for D&T. The notion, and it was a very good one, was that a particular process, for example joining pieces of wood together, which would be used in the main part of a design and make project, would be introduced, experimented with and practised in advance of the main phase of the work. Children would be able to perfect an operation which they would make use of later. There is no reason why this approach cannot be employed in a similar, but less practical context. The skills involved in extracting understanding from the Internet can indeed be practised in advance. Some of the approaches above lend themselves well to this sort of use.

Example of an Internet-based Focused Practical task

Practising with a KWL Grid

As a precursor to some extended research work in which the teacher wanted to make use of the KWL grid as a means of encouraging a high level of engagement with the topic and of generating interest in the work, a short exercise in the use of the grid, which was entirely new to the class was used. The topic of Henry VIII was chosen for two reasons: first it was totally unrelated to the main area of research which the class would move on to investigate; and secondly it was a topic which had been covered in depth in the previous school year.

The session started with what we will call a 'Thought Trawl' (variously known as Brainstorm – now considered inappropriate by some because of its medical associations; Mind Shower; Ideas Meet and so on). Children were asked simply to express any idea or fact or thought relating to Henry VIII and his era. This worked well and the class were next asked to choose three ideas, either of their own, or taken from the board where the ideas had been recorded. The ideas were written into the first column of a KWL grid.

This short time of ideas and comments from the class and the opportunity for all of them to be refreshed in their knowledge of the topic was capitalised upon and the children were asked to formulate three questions which they did not know the answers to, but which they would like to find out. Help was given with the style of question to ask and importance was given to the likelihood of being able to find the answer. The teacher asked, for example, if the class thought that it would be possible to find the colour of Henry VIII's eyes, or whether as a family the King and wives had pets. Direction at this stage was deemed important. The children really needed to be thinking about what interested them, but also needed to be directed away from patently simplistic, or patently very difficult to answer, questions. The children were offered the opportunity to work with a partner for the formulation of the questions and many took up this offer; some preferred to continue alone. With the questions in place, the teacher distributed three different photocopied sources – two pages from a history book, a direct copy of a website written for children and an altered transcript from a website designed for older investigators. The text from the third source had been simplified, made larger and set out in a more appealing and easy-to-read way.

To keep the activity short and to allow time for a discussion of the process and to listen to some of the answers, the teacher asked the class to find the answer to just one question, or possibly two if time allowed. Just before the work began the teacher gave out coloured highlighter pens and suggested that as they looked through the writing (the word 'read' was avoided at this stage to encourage the idea of skimming through the text) they should use the highlighter to mark words, sentences of short passages which gave information related to the question which they were reminded to keep firmly in mind.

The children were asked to make very brief notes, which, in conjunction with the highlighted sections on the pages, they would be able to use to write an answer to the question which they had originally posed. For this particular task they were not going to be asked to write answers, but simply find and record the information which would help them to write answers in good prose style at a later point if necessary. This was another way of keeping the activity short and not too onerous. For about fifteen minutes the class were left to explore the texts, the teacher circulated and offered help or joined in discussions as seemed appropriate.

At the end of the time of activity the class were brought back together and asked to give verbal reports and answers to the questions which had been posed. This was a lively time of contributions and some contradiction. The teacher wanted to end the session with a little reflection of the process and to elicit the children's thoughts about the use of the KWL as a means to improving and simplifying the research work. Some of the responses were interesting:

> 'I'd forgotten that we did Henry the Eighth.'
>
> 'It made me stick to my question.'
>
> 'You couldn't always use one [*a KWL grid*], but it helps you know what to do when you get started.'

The comments here show that these children at least found that the use of the grid helped with creating and keeping to a clear focus, and that as an introductory tool it was useful. These responses, and some of the others not included here, illustrate a measure of metacognition which the teacher was keen to encourage. The children were prompted towards thinking about the process of their learning and how the use of the grid might have had an impact on it.

So, as a practice run with the use of a KWL grid, the teacher was pleased with the way that the class had worked. As a short 'focused practical task' it had served its purpose. The children had experienced the reactivation of their pre-existing knowledge, though they probably did not express it in that way, they had chosen an area to concentrate on and they had engaged with different texts to find and extract relevant pieces of information. The stage was set to put the newly acquired strategy into use on a wider topic.

Working with Words from the Internet: Keep it short and make a comment

The temptation to cut and paste long passages from electronic sources can be overwhelming. One way to begin to discourage this is to introduce some guidelines, or simple rules.

Quite young children, at the beginning of Key Stage One, are perfectly capable of using the technical skills needed to extract text, and pictures, from Internet sites. As soon as they begin doing this they need to be taught that there are both good and bad approaches to this kind of work. To take large passages and paste them into a document is bad, to use a short extract and to write personal comments or reflections is good.

Three simple rules which can be introduced and the rationale for them simply explained are:

- keep any extract short;
- explain why you chose the extract, or write something of your own about it;
- make sure you say where the extract came from.

The rationale for this guidance is as follows:

Keep any extract short: By keeping the quote from a website short, the end product will be less likely to be made up entirely of passages taken directly from the source. Being obliged to make a selection from a longer passage necessitates reading and the making of decisions about which part to select. Reading the information, instead of finding a 'chunk' and using the whole piece, means that the children will engage at some level with the text.

Explain why you chose the extract, or write something of your own about it: This rule can be followed in at least two different ways. The comment could be the child's reason for including the quote, for example: '*This sentence tells us that there is no wind on the moon.*' or '*I included this because it tells us about the first blow-up* *tyres for bikes.'* An alternative style of comment could be concerned with something more personal: *'My dad says that his first bike was a Penny Farthing, but I don't believe that because he was born in 1968.'* The purpose of this rule is similar to the purpose of the first. It is an attempt to encourage children to engage with the text. This rule also encourages the child to think more broadly about the extract and to give it a context.

Say where the information came from: This rule is to encourage honesty about where ideas and information have come from, and to encourage clarity about the difference between their work and the work of somebody else. It is hoped that applying this rule will lead to good habits, and help to avoid unintentional plagiarism.

The rules apply equally to long or short pieces of work. The two examples below illustrate the idea well, they were written by children in Key Stage One as part of an ICT-based project on finding information. They both illustrate a short extract, a comment, both personal and reflective, and the source of the extract is acknowledged.

Figure 3.2 *Information-finding about D-day*

D-day

The Germans concentrated their troops near Calais, at the narrowest part of the English Channel. But the Allies planned to land farther west, in a region of northern France called Normandy.

Eisenhower chose Monday, June 5, 1944, as D-Day, the date of the Normandy invasion.

This is from Information Finder, a CD at school. We looked up Normandy and found lots of information. I have been to Normandy and seen the beach called Omaha, the soldiers landed there in 1944. The soldiers tricked the Germans by going to Normandy instead of Calais.

D-day was the start of England winning the war. If it had gone wrong we would not have won the war.

Figure 3.3 *Information-finding about the moon landing*

Landing a Space Rocket on the Moon

On July 20, 1969, U.S. astronauts Neil A. Armstrong and Edwin E. Aldrin, Jr., landed the Apollo 11 lunar module on the moon. Armstrong became the first person to set foot on the moon.

This was 30 years ago and my dad says that everyone watched it on the television. It is like a special day for me because it is very near my birthday. His footprints are still on the moon because there is no wind.

I found this on the school CD called Information Finder. I did a search with James for Apollo, because we knew the name of the rocket.

Working with Words from the Internet: the 'Text Explanation Sheet'

In many cases the information that can be found on an Internet site is interesting, informative and holds the answers to questions that have been posed. However, very often the format of the information, the style of the language, and other factors make it less than accessible for some primary-aged children. Keeping in mind the need for children to engage with the content of their work, and the need to keep interest levels high, the 'Text Explanation Sheet' can have a useful role.

In a sense the sheet is a simple writing frame, but it is the nature of the task that it leads to which is particularly useful. The sheet is set out with a series of headings, and the children are asked to complete it, the aim being to produce an audience-friendly product. The particular audience can be different according to the aims of the work in question. Often to produce an information sheet for younger children to use is an effective activity. This is true especially if the younger children in question are known – perhaps in a paired class situation where a class of older children are matched with a class of younger children and where activities, such as reading, are sometimes shared. If the older children have been asked to investigate the type of reading material which seems to appeal to the younger children, the end products can be even better.

The headings on the sheet should include:

- a title;
- a space for original text – taken directly from the electronic source;
- a glossary;
- a space for comments.

The idea is that a short extract from a website is taken directly and its source acknowledged, any interesting or difficult words are explained, and the text is modified and added to, just a little, in order to make it accessible and understandable to the new audience. The precise layout of the sheet is not important, but clear guidance and reminders need to be given if the most is to be made of the activity. Naturally there are many variations on this activity, but the constant feature is that the children undertaking it are obliged to think carefully about the wording and content and also to think about the meanings of words, then in some cases consult other sources of reference – a dictionary for example. More or less emphasis can be placed upon the comments section. To give some thoughts or reflections, or to relate what is contained in the original text to a personal experience is a sound way to encourage engagement.

The examples below are from upper primary-aged children writing, in 'Native American Indians' for others of the same age, and in 'The First Cheap Car', for children two years younger.

Table 3.5 Text explanation sheet

Native American Indians **Sarah C. and Emma S. 6P**

Native American Indians were the original inhabitants of North America. Canada and the USA are the two countries of North America.

[Original inhabitants: The first ones to live there.]

1. The Navajo Indians

> **Navajo,** Native American people of the Athabascan language family and of the Southwest culture area. The Navajo live on reservations in northeastern Arizona and contiguous parts of New Mexico and Utah. They are closely related to the Apache and originally emigrated from areas to the north. It is thought that they settled in the southwest during the 16th century. By the 17th century the Navajo had become a pastoral people, with an economy based largely on herding and hunting.
> **Encarta – Search for Native Indians then choose related articles then choose Navajo.**

The Navajo Indians live in the south-west of the USA. They live on reservations. The reservations are in the states of Arizona, New Mexico and Utah. The Navajo Indians are related to the Apache Indians. The Navajo Indians lived by keeping animals and hunting.
[Reservations: special parts of the country given to Native American Indians.]

2. The Apache Indians

> **Apache,** group of six culturally related Native American peoples descended from Athabascan-speaking nations. The various peoples are: the Kiowa Apache, who lived between the northern border of New Mexico and the Platte River; the Lipan of eastern New Mexico and western Texas; the Jicarilla of southern New Mexico; the Mescalero of central New Mexico; the Chiricahua of the Chiricahua mountain range in southwestern Arizona; and the Western Apache of central Arizona. They were primarily hunters of buffalo, but they also practised farming to a limited degree. For centuries they were fierce warriors, adept in desert survival, carrying out raids on those who encroached on their territory.
> **Encarta – Search for Apache.**

The Apache Indians are a big tribe made up of six smaller tribes. They live in New Mexico, Arizona and Texas. The Apaches hunted for buffaloes and they were also farmers. They were good fighters too. They would fight with anyone who came on their land.

[Tribe: like a very big family of families all living and working together.]

Geronimo. A famous Apache leader.

Table 3.6 Text explanation sheet

Explaining the Text or 'So what's this all about then?'

The First Cheap Car
Jamie C. and Sarah H.

Text from ... The Encarta website
In 1908 Detroit car manufacturer Henry Ford produced the first Model T Ford, a car that revolutionised the motor industry. The car was inexpensive, enabling the average person to become a car owner. With the model T, spare parts and repairs became rapidly available for the first time. Henry Ford also revolutionised the process of industrial production. The car was built on an assembly line, where different workers handled the different aspects of manufacture as the car passed along the line. The technique was soon adopted by many other industries.

Glossary or 'What does that mean?'
1. **revolutionised**: this means made a very big change to something.
2. **assembly**: this can mean putting things together.
3. **manufacture**: this means making things in a factory.
4. **inexpensive**: this means cheap.

Comments on the text
This writing is about the first person to use a production line. The car moves along and different people work on it as it goes by. The people always do the same job, like put the wheels on, or fit the seats. All car factories use production lines now.
Jamie:

The model T Ford is a very small car. I've seen one at the British Road Transport Museum.

Sarah:

My Grandad used to work on an assembly line at Massey Ferguson where they make tractors. He put wheels on and he said that it is boring doing the same thing all day.

Communications

There is an important aspect to the use of ICT in schools which so far we have not really explored. It is concerned with the communications aspect of ICT. Many involved in the use of the new technologies in schools feel strongly that the communications capabilities of the Internet are most likely to lead to long-term and radical shifts in the way that education is approached as we move further into the 21st century.

There are examples from as far back as the 1980s of children communicating through e-mail. Originally contacts were made between classes of children much in the same way as letters have been exchanged over the years and links developed via the Royal Mail. As time has passed and technology progressed, communications projects have developed into such realms as 'Ask an Expert' (see for example: http://www.askanexpert.com/; this site acts as a clearing house for the numerous sites offering free help with an enormous range of topics). Children are invited to ask a question of an expert in the field, a working scientist, for example an archaeologist or an author. The questions are not usually answered immediately, but within a given time frame. On some of the sites there are question archives where all previous questions are stored in a searchable database. There seems to have been an expansion of this service related to revision for public exams – SATs, GCSEs, AS and A levels. This is something which some teachers build into their classwork as a way of learning about and gaining from Internet communications, and of dealing with certain content-based questions from National Curriculum subjects.

A very successful project with simple communications technology was reported by Ipgrave (2002). In her exploration of dialogue in the Religious Education classroom she describes an e-mail project which led to a very high level of dialogue on the subject of cultural and religious differences between children in two Leicestershire schools in very different socio-economic and cultural/religious settings. One school had a high proportion of children from an Asian background. Questions concerning the meaning of 'mass', and the activities of 'Eid' were asked and answered with a simplicity and naturalness that might be difficult to generate by any other means. Had the children met face to face with similar aims, it is very unlikely that the type and quality of question would have been equalled, even with detailed preparation. Shyness and other hiccoughs would have been very likely to undermine the event. Both the immediacy and, strangely, the opportunity for pause for thought before replying served to make the project a success.

Professor Stephen Heppell (Heppell 2003) at the University of East Anglia's Ultralab talks about symmetry in communications, and gives examples from technology of text messaging with mobile phones, and e-mail as forms of communication which allow for an equality of participation, that is, there is not one-way traffic. The communication function is not restricted to an incoming flow of information and there is great scope for interaction, exchange and dialogue. This is an aspect of the Internet which can be, but should not be, neglected. E-mail projects are relatively straightforward to plan and organise and the results can be very good, generating a great amount of interest and excitement from those involved.

CHAPTER 4

Using numbers and number activities from the Internet

With the risk of repeating the ideas in the initial sentences from the previous chapter, it is worth reminding ourselves of the vast range and variety of sites accessible via the Internet. Many of them contain statistical data which is real, up to date and sometimes complex.

These sites can provide the raw material for both mathematical tasks and for other tasks concerned with investigations in other subject areas. They can be very useful in classroom learning situations. Many of these sites share the features which can assist in the process of encouraging effective learning; some by the very nature of the information being Internet-based, and others by the nature of the data and the use to which it might be put in the classroom.

We have seen that, in general terms, the Internet is motivating. It is, very often, culturally and socially appropriate, leads to authentic learning tasks and can stimulate the type of social interaction which is so important if effective learning is to take place.

In this chapter we will look at some of the ways in which children can be encouraged to engage in tasks which make use of and rely upon numbers and statistical information, in different formats and in different subject areas, from the Internet.

It is important to consider the difference between an activity which is delivered via the medium of the Internet, but could be undertaken in another computer-mediated way, and Internet activities which could not easily be undertaken without the Internet. What this means is that there are many sites which simply have software which is accessible and can be used via the Internet. The same software is often available for purchase, or can be downloaded free and can be used without a connection to the Internet. Whatever the program encourages children to do, does not need access to the Internet and so the work is not, in the sense that we are considering here, Internet dependent. There are, for example, sites with a selection of mathematical activities that can be used while connected to the Internet; the same programs could be used (given their availability) without the use of the Internet. The consideration with these programs, which teachers must make, is whether or not the activities are likely to help achieve the learning objectives set for the children in question. Certainly the Internet is a rich source of activities, many of which meet the specific needs which a teacher might have in mind. It is possible that the activity accessed via the Internet does meet the requirements of interest, context, ability to work collaboratively and so on, but it would do all of these things if it were not found on the Internet, but on a CD-ROM. The point here is that there is a difference between what might be considered more routine, non-Internet-dependent activity carried out with a computer, and activities which rely on the access to information and other resources which would not be nearly so accessible without the Internet. The example later in this chapter, investigating the speeds of different animals, does not rely on an activity mediated through the Internet, but relies on access to information. It exemplifies an investigation which can be tackled, with some speed and accuracy, with reference to the Internet and to developing Internet handling skills. In the process of the investigation mathematical content is handled, and mathematical skills are put to use and practised. This is an example of using numbers from the Internet in order to encourage work in mathematics in a highly applied and contextualised way.

Using the Internet to Support Learning in Mathematics

If we look at the use of numbers in teaching there will obviously be a strong bias towards the teaching of mathematics. For this reason we will briefly explore the ways in which computer use, in general, is considered to support learning in mathematics, looking specifically at what the Internet can provide in this context.

The National Council for Educational Technology (NCET now the British Educational Communications Technology Agency – BECTa) (NCET 1997) set out what they term major opportunities which the use of Information Technology is able to provide to support learning in mathematics:

- *learning* from feedback;
- *observing* patterns;
- *exploring* data;
- *teaching* the computer;
- *developing* visual imagery.

It is worthy of note that the use of a computer for repeated practice ('drill and practice'), largely a behaviouristic approach, is not considered a major opportunity here.

Learning from Feedback

- When children are asked to carry out any sort of activity they will expect and actually require some sort of feedback as a part of the learning process. Particular Internet sites are very good at providing constructive feedback.
- A computer can give impartial, non-judgemental feedback, and will never tire of doing so. The feedback which is available when using a variety of Internet-based activities, in conjunction with the facility to make changes very easily, encourage children to conjecture and hypothesise, to try out ideas and to use an approach which is both problem-solving and risk taking.
- Approaches which rely on what is sometimes called trial and error depend heavily upon feedback. Certain Internet-based uses, and also the use of other software and calculators, are extremely well suited to providing feedback.

Observing Patterns

- Looking for and finding patterns in numbers and other mathematical situations is fundamental to the development of an understanding of many of the foundations of mathematics.
- The Programmes of Study for both Key Stages One and Two outline the need to teach children about patterns in numbers and shapes.

For example:

'Key Stage 1

2. Pupils should be taught to: . . .

(b) create and describe number patterns; explore and record patterns related to addition and subtraction, and then patterns of multiples of 2, 5 and 10 explaining the patterns and using them to make predictions; recognise sequences, including odd and even numbers to 30 then beyond; recognise the relationship between halving and doubling.'

And:

'Key Stage 2

2. Pupils should be taught to: . . .

(b) recognise and describe number patterns, including two- and three-digit multiples of 2, 5 or 10, recognising their patterns and using these to make predictions; make general statements, using words to describe a functional relationship, and test these; recognise prime numbers to 20 and square numbers up to 10 × 10; find factor pairs and all the prime factors of any two-digit integer.'

(QCA 2000)

- In the Key Objectives of the National Numeracy Strategy (NNS) (DfEE 1999b) the recognition and recreation of simple patterns is listed for Reception, and in successive years great reliance is placed on the use of patterns to help in the carrying out of arithmetical operations and in the solving of all types of mathematical problems.
- The Internet is, again, a rich source of material for use in this respect. The use of a spreadsheet with collected data is an ideal developmental activity.

Exploring Data

- The use of real data in examples for children to work with always used to be problematic. If numbers have to be manipulated without recourse to technology, then it is sensible to keep the numbers simple, preferably whole, and secondly to keep the number of examples to a minimum.
- Real data collected from real situations give a meaning to work, which somebody else's contrived or remote data does not. The use of real, relevant and appropriate data is an excellent starting point if the all-important engagement is to be established and the Internet can provide this data. Not only can it provide the 'raw' data, but it can also provide the setting for suitable activities with the data; in some cases the interactivity and possibilities for communication are the factors which take the planned activity to higher levels of success in terms of the achievement of the planned learning outcomes.

Teaching the Computer

- Teaching the computer is perhaps not usually associated with Internet provision. The use of Logo is the best example of this learning opportunity, and the use of Logo does not rely upon the Internet. However there are other activities which involve the giving of instructions and making use of feedback which can be accessed via the Internet.
- In Logo, Seymour Papert (e.g. Papert 1982) uses an analogy with teaching to explain how children develop short pieces of program which, when run, will carry out a particular operation: draw a triangle for example. In this sense, the computer has been taught to draw the triangle and the child has to write instructions that are clear and unambiguous. Children take on responsibility

for their own work and actions in this environment and they are encouraged to take risks and to experiment.

Developing Visual Imagery

- Children, in most cases, benefit from some visual element in their learning.
- The proverb about hearing and forgetting, seeing and remembering and doing and understanding comes to mind again here. For example, if children are able to see shapes, build shapes, carry out transformations on shapes on a computer screen, they are able to take these images and construct their own knowledge of shapes. It is highly likely that they will come to a deeper understanding of shapes and their relationships to one another, than if they had only experienced a static version of the same phenomena. Again, the Internet is certainly not unique in its ability to provide opportunity for developing visual imagery, but there are more opportunities available on the Internet than could be easily available to a teacher using a stand-alone, non-Internet-connected computer.

Away from the realm of learning in mathematics, there are also many opportunities to make use of numbers, facts and figures, to support the development of understanding in many other subject contexts. There are many official, i.e. government-owned sites that provide statistics about absolutely everything that can be quantified. In Great Britain, the Office for National Statistics (to be found at: www.statistics.gov.uk/) plays the role of provider of facts and figures. Each government department also has a branch dealing with the facts and figures relating to the responsibility of the department.

So, for example, any details of such things as population growth (The Population Reference Bureau: www.prb.org/), new car sales (www.statistics.gov.uk/), the number of homes with digital televisions (www.itc.org.uk/), computer provision in schools, (www.dfes.gov.uk/statistics/) can always be found somewhere on the Internet.

Investigations, Surveys and Answering Questions

An Investigation to Consider

There are many different ways of beginning investigations. Some investigations are simply given, i.e. the children are told what, and often how, to investigate. In other cases investigations can develop from work which has been carried out and teachers can encourage the asking of further questions and the planning of investigations of different types.

An example of an investigation using numbers from the Internet could involve any subject. In this example, in the context of work from the National Curriculum

History Programmes of Study, children have been learning about Ancient Greece (A European History Study: DfEE/QCA 1999a, p.106). The Olympic Games have been touched upon, linked to work in P.E. lessons where an Athletics Award Scheme is being followed. The class are asked to find out about how records for particular events have changed over the years. The task is left open-ended deliberately, although the teacher is aware that certain children will need greater support and direction and the intention is to give specific tasks to carry out to some of the pairs of children in this category. The simplest task of this type will be to construct a graph showing the improvement in performance of a single event. The teacher will provide access to a site where Olympic records are listed. For others in the class the work will be less prescriptive and will involve initial investigation and then the planning of a focused piece of work.

The teacher prepared a briefing sheet for the majority of the class to use and some time was spent looking at particular ideas which could be followed up though the teacher was conscious that by presenting particular ideas, aspects of personal interest or creativity may be stifled.

Table 4.1 Teacher's briefing sheet (for most children)

The Olympic Games Through the Years
a look at some statistics

!!! REMINDER !!!

Use Ask Jeeves for Kids as a starting point:
http://www.ajkids.com/
If you have trouble finding a good site you can try:
http://www.perseus.tufts.edu/Olympics/

You should include the following:

1. The start of the Olympic Games – a short introduction.
2. Three Amazing Facts – find three odd or unusual facts from the history of the games.
3. Your Special Investigation – choose something from the history of the whole games and use the facts and figures that you find to present the findings of your work.

Examples of what you could investigate:

—Do the records for each event improve at every games?
—Which events have improved the most since the beginning of the modern Olympic Games?
—Have men and women improved the same as each other over the years?
—Have records for throwing, jumping, sprinting, middle distance, or long distance improved the most since the beginning of the modern games?

***

You must present your work clearly and neatly in a separate topic folder.

***

For the investigation you must say exactly what it is that you have investigated and the way in which your investigation was carried out.

***

You will need to make good use of charts and graphs to show your findings.

***

Table 4.2 Teacher's briefing sheet (less prescriptive)

The Olympic Games Through the Years
a look at some statistics

!!! REMINDER !!!

Go to 'The History of the Modern Olympic Games' page at
http://www.slb.com/seed/en/watch/olympics/history.htm
Print out the page and use a highlighter pen to help you with these questions:

1. Where did the Olympic Games first take place?
2. What were the sports in the original Olympic Games?
3. When did the 'Modern Olympic Games' begin?

Use the printed sheet and what you have highlighted to write answers.

Choose an event and make a list of the records for it for all of the modern games. You will find the records at this site:
http://www.ex.ac.uk/cimt/data/olympics/olymindx.htm

Draw a bar chart for the records for the event which you have chosen.

Write about your bar chart. Is there anything unusual about any part of it?

If there is time you can choose another event to look at in detail.

For a group of lower ability children the more basic requirements were still too advanced. For these children the teacher prepared a shortened list of records for two events and asked them to draw simple bar charts. They were also given five short sentences to complete about the history of the games, based on a simple text taken from a children's history site, found via: http://www.livinglibrary.co.uk/.

This top of Key Stage Two investigation makes high demands on the children. The need for teacher support across the ability range was high, but the resulting reports were of a uniformly high standard.

The most able children were able to work with limited support, though the teacher did spend time at the beginning ensuring, through explanation and questioning, that these particular children had a very clear picture of what was to be done. The level of intervention with these children was low in comparison to the middle and lower ability groups in the class. The briefing sheet for the more able did not mention the use of a highlighter pen, but it was interesting to see that in one or two cases this was a preferred method of working. The demands made of the mathematical abilities of these children were high, and in some ways the statistical elements of the final pieces of work were the weakest part. It was noticeable that there was a clear crossover from work in numeracy lessons dealing with graphical representation and percentages, although there was need for some direct help with some of this. With the most able there was a tendency towards being sidetracked. Asking children to use a search engine, instead of giving them sites to visit directly, will always lead to this possibility. However the teacher considered that experience with one or more different search engines was important at this stage for these particular children. Some of the group actually found it useful to visit the sites provided for the rest of the class, and abandoned their searches after a while.

After a slow start the middle ability group settled to work well. Again, some considerable time was spent going through the briefing sheet, and making it clear what was to be done. The language of the briefing sheet was, deliberately, at a higher level than some of the children were easily able to work with. This was designed to encourage discussion and questioning in the initial stages, and in the initial discussion children were told to make notes on the sheets to make them clearer. The teacher had intended to form the pairs herself, ensuring that a more able reader would be paired with a less able reader. In the event this did not happen.

In some ways the tasks set for the least able children in the class were the most successful. These children produced work which satisfied the requirements set by the teacher and of which the children were rightly pleased. The production of bar charts took some time, many were eventually drawn by hand after some difficulties with the graph-drawing software. The more able children in the class were expected to make use of the spreadsheet Excel, and this worked well. Some of the lower ability children were able to use Excel on the occasions when a classroom assistant was available, but the use was limited to transferring what had already been accomplished on paper to a spreadsheet and producing graphs.

If we look back to the principles listed at the end of Chapter Two, we can reference the Olympics project against them and see how good a fit is made.

1. Learners need enough previous knowledge and understanding to enable them to learn new things.

The introductory work on which the Olympics work was based used the preceding weeks' work on the topic of Ancient Greece. This topic was developed on the principle that the children had some previous knowledge concerning the Ancient World, based partly upon the reading of some simplified Greek Myths, and partly upon what individual children brought with them from their experience of life – travel, books, films and so on. The concentration on the sporting side of ancient Greek life, the particular activities and the development of the advent of the 'games', developed out of the more general work on Ancient Greece, and was related to what was actually happening in the children's P.E. lessons at the time. At the same time as working for an award scheme, the teacher had organised, in preparation, an Ancient Olympic-style pentathlon competition. Put together, all of these experiences gave a good foundation for the ensuing work to be built upon.

2. Provision should be made for social interaction and discussion in groups of varying sizes, both with and without the teacher.

As a feature of much of the work in this particular classroom, class discussion formed an important and regular part of the introduction and subsequent development of the work. At the outset discussion, based upon what had already been covered and upon what the children could contribute from elsewhere, formed the mainstay of the introduction. Children were encouraged to contribute, to listen and to comment on the contributions of others. As the work proceeded, by working in pairs, discussion was encouraged. The teacher set aside a time at the end of each lesson when each pair was expected to feedback on the work to date. This was often only a short time when pairs simply said what they had done, what they had discovered and from where. On occasion the reporting back of one pair led to interest and questions from others.

3. Meaningful contexts for learning are very important.

The setting for this work has, partly, been considered in the first point above. By considering the children's prior knowledge, the setting was strengthened. The context was one part of the realm of Ancient Greece, paired with a more modern context, that of participation in modern athletics in school.

4. Children's awareness of their own thought processes should be promoted.

This is perhaps more difficult to see. There was an attempt to make this happen in two particular cases though. Firstly the use of highlighter pens, something which was not new to the children, was, in part designed to encourage them to think more about how to approach the answers to questions, rather than simply cutting and pasting a sentence which might or might not answer the question effectively. The reasons for this approach was explained to the children and in general they used the method well. In some cases entire passages from the printed websites were highlighted which did not really serve the intended purpose. Secondly in the end of lesson feedback plenaries, the teacher encouraged the children to make their reasons for certain courses of action clear to the class. For example, some of the methods used for calculating the differences in performance over time were, to say the least, a little idiosyncratic. Making the method and the reasoning behind the method explicit seemed to give opportunities for individuals to rethink what they had done, and in some cases gave pointers to others.

A Survey to Undertake

Volcano Activity

At the end of the Autumn Term a child brought in a small newspaper cutting about a volcanic eruption in Nicaragua. This was related to an extract from a story which the teacher had read to the class as a part of shared reading in a literacy lesson. The teacher had not asked for anything to be brought in nor had she planned to follow up the volcano story, but she actually followed the interest sparked by the story and the newspaper cutting and planned a short volcano survey at the start of the next term. The aim of the volcano survey was to illustrate that volcanoes are not simply an aspect of history, but a part of everyday life for many people in many parts of the world.

For the start of the Spring Term a world map was prepared and the site of the Nicaragua volcano – San Christabel, which had erupted in the previous December – was plotted. The plan which the teacher had made was to spend a few minutes each day with the class looking at a volcano website (www.volcanoworld.org/) which reports worldwide volcanic activity as it happens. Based on the state of activity each day, or most likely less frequently than that, the position of the volcano would be noted and marked on the map and a sentence or two of explanation would be written and pinned to the board next to the map. Each day a different pair of children would be responsible for checking the Internet for eruptions!

During the Spring Term a total of 15 volcanic eruptions worldwide were logged on the website, and subsequently plotted on the classroom map and written about by the 'duty pair' for the day. By the end of the term the interest was no less than it had been at the start of the term and the engagement with a range of new ideas and skills had been high.

To conclude the survey and to bring together all of the different ideas that had been discussed concerning volcanoes, the teacher planned to spend a 'Volcano Day' during the last week of the term. The emphasis of the day would be on the numbers which the children had come across during the term, since it was the numbers which some of the children seemed puzzled by. Such ideas as 'plume height', and 'volume' had been encountered, and discussed briefly, but the teacher wanted to use these examples of rather large numbers to help the children understand the concepts involved a little better.

Plume height ranging from about 100 metres, a size which could just about be grasped by the class, to 'greater than 25 kilometres' which, even when considered in terms of distance from place to place on land, was beyond the understanding of most children.

During the day each child, working with a partner, spent time drawing a large representation of the eruptions which had taken place during the term, according to the size of the eruption. This required them to place the eruptions in magnitude order and then to work on a suitable scale to ensure that their diagrams would fit on to the A2-sized paper which they were given to use. A good deal of help was given with this work.

Other activities to complete during the day were to be chosen from a set of options. The activities focused on numbers, scale and size and were:

- find out about the biggest eruption that you can and draw a diagram to represent it;

- find out how fast lava can travel; would it break the speed limit?
- find out how many volcanoes erupt each day, week, month and year;
- draw a volcano time line starting with Vesuvius; put other important events on the time line too.

In practice the time line was attempted by none of the class, but all of the other activities were undertaken; some pairs completed all three of them.

In keeping with an end of term feeling, the following afternoon the children were introduced to a set of games on the Volcano World website (http://volcano.und.nodak.edu/vwdocs/kids/fun/fun.html).

Some interesting descriptive words were also encountered: *non-explosive, gentle, explosive, severe, cataclysmic, paroxysmal, colossal, super-colossal, mega-colossal.* These words describe the size of an eruption and formed the basis of a set of diagrams which the children devised.

For a long, though not highly time-consuming, project which culminated in a day or so of intensive work, this was judged to be successful. For the most part logging the eruptions took less than five or ten minutes on each occasion, and the time spent at the end of the term, time which was not accounted for in any of the formal medium-term plans for the class, was time well spent in the view of the teacher. The work had generated a good deal of interest. Other newspaper cuttings, and a range of Internet-based pictures and other information joined the original cutting in what became an expansive wall display. The partial concentration on the numbers associated with the collection of information led well into numeracy related topics, and examples for the volcano work served to illustrate and supply raw data in numeracy lessons. By the same token, work covered in numeracy lessons was applied in a contrasting and useful context.

Given the chance that led to this work, and linked with the fact that it originated from an interest of one child in the class, we can see that context, interest and motivation were key factors in its success.

The mini-project was based on a little, but a growing, bank of prior knowledge, the context was hit upon by the children themselves, since the initial introduction to volcanoes in a literacy lesson clearly fired the imaginations of at least some of the class. Collaborative work was a feature throughout, and whole-class involvement was high, especially on the occasions when there was an eruption to report and to find out about.

Some Questions to Answer

In the context of a topic dealing with animals from around the world a class of children in the lower part of Key Stage Two were given a free hand and asked to develop a mini-presentation dealing with a particular aspect of the topic which was of interest to them.

This part of the work was divided into three. First the individual children were asked to choose an aspect of the topic which was of interest to them, next they decided upon some simple questions to find answers for, followed by a presentation of their answers to the class. The third phase entailed the class offering suggestions for further questions to explore. This next stage of questioning was guided initially by the teacher who attempted to keep the follow-up questions reasonable and answerable. The aim was to develop some questions for each child which would involve more than the finding-out of facts. The initial questions to answer would lead to a narrower field of enquiry and questions in need of more than a simple factual answer. The further questions would add a dimension of investigation to the work, and would ideally lead to the need for a strategy to be put in place which would involve more 'working out' to be done. The notion of working out implies, for many, the use of figures, and arithmetic, and this, in deed, was a part of the aim of the work in question. If possible the teacher wanted to apply, in a context away from the numeracy lesson, some of the number skills which the children possessed, and possibly develop them further.

The example below shows how the process developed for one child. Four sections of an introductory sheet were in need of completion. The 'Questions from the class' would not be completed until the initial questions had been answered and the answers given to the group.

Table 4.3 A child's mini-presentation

The World of Animals by Sammy J.

My Interests:
Big and Dangerous Cats

What I know about Big and Dangerous Cats:
I think the leopard is the fastest runner and they catch little deer to eat.

My Questions:
How fast can the fastest cat run?
How fast can we run?
How slow is the slowest animal?

Questions from the class:
How long would it take the fastest animal to get to school?
How long would it take the slowest animal to get to school?

Sammy's progress was as follows. Since he was familiar with Internet searching the teacher allowed him to search for the answers to his questions without any restrictions. Other children in the mixed-age class who were not so adept with search engines were given appropriate help. For example, the teacher carried out initial searches and presented them with one, or sometimes more than one, website to investigate.

Sammy's first search, with the search engine Yahooligans (www.yahooligans.com) did not satisfy him. He was presented with a list of potential sites and categories to explore but as he did not immediately come across the answer to his question at the first two sites which he tried, he choose to change search engine and tried Google for Kids and Teens (http://directory.google.com/Top/Kids_and_Teens/). Sammy's search for Leopards in this engine again produced a set of categories for him to choose from. On looking through the categories he complained to the enquiring teacher that they were no good and didn't include anything about speed. This may or may not have been the case, but for Sammy, who felt let down by his searches, the answer was to try a whole web search with Google, rather than a restricted 'kids and teens' search. The search on the keyword 'leopard' yielded over 900,000 hits and he began to start looking at the sites in order. The teacher, again on hand to intervene, suggested narrowing the search, a concept not new to Sammy, and between them they decided to search for two key words, 'leopard' and 'mph'. The number of sites on the next list was still large: 4,616, but the seventh site on the list – Killer Cats: An Exhibit about Cats in the Wild – grabbed his attention and at this site he was able to find the answers to his questions. He actually spent a long time browsing the site and making notes in his rough book about other points which took his attention. He found that the cheetah could outrun the leopard, with a top speed of nearly double the leopard's 40 mph.

Answering his next two questions took a little longer, but with a suggestion from the teacher, who thought that perhaps a snail might be the slowest moving creature, he was able to find a chart which set out the speeds of a range of different animals including the human variety. The first search with Google with the keyword 'snail' netted over one million hits. This was refined by adding the keyword 'mph' (again) and of the 4,000 plus sites listed, two on the first page included what was being looked for. The first one: http://www.teach-at-home.com/fastfacts/animalkingdom/Speed.asp had a list of land, sea and air creatures' top speeds, and the second: www.doghause.com/funfacts03.html had a similar list of just the land animals.

The charts on both sites confirmed the cheetah as the fastest, put the garden snail at the slowest, but the thee-toed sloth, an animal new to Sammy, was only marginally faster and took his interest.

The first three questions were now answered:

Fastest cat: cheetah: 70 mph

Human top speed: either 27.89 mph, or 23 mph, according to which source was consulted. (This could be cause for concern, and could be followed up but Sammy was happy to use both figures and live with the fact that there is conflicting information available.)

Slowest animal: garden snail 0.03 mph; but more interestingly, three-toed sloth 0.15 mph

When the answers to his questions were presented to the class, in a simple two-minute talk (which lasted only slightly more than 30 seconds in reality), the class seemed to be taken with the slowness of the snail and sloth, and several children suggested that it would take a very long time to 'Get to your holiday', or 'Get home from school.' Other suggestions on this theme led to the formulation of the next questions to be tackled. With a little help from the teacher Sammy had the following questions to pursue:

- How long would it take the fastest animal to get to school?
- How long would it take the slowest animal to get to school?

To answer these two apparently simple questions took a little more time. The process began with looking for a map of the local area. Surprisingly the A to Z map that was in the school was too old to have the streets of the recently built estate. The Internet provided the solution here too. There are a number of map sites which can zoom into the level of the street, allow for printing and obviously provide the scale. (For example: both www.mapquest.co.uk/ and www.streetmap.co.uk/ allow for a street name, or a post code to be entered in order to find the appropriate map.) With some intricate measuring and some basic calculation, the timings of the journeys to and from school were calculated and the cause of much interest and amusement.

In this example both factual questions and questions based on the facts but in need of more thought and investigation were answered. Some of the principles outlined earlier clearly came into play in this example. The work was set in a context of interest to the children. The context was not necessarily of the children's first-hand experience, but the interest in animals and the work undertaken in preceding lessons set the scene well. The children were able to follow their own particular interests. Although essentially working alone, the reporting back to the class and the support offered brought in a socially constructive aspect to the work. The layout of the first sheet for the children to complete had a short section that encouraged them to think about their current knowledge. In Sammy's case his 'knowledge' was actually flawed however.

It is worthy of note here that the teacher's plans did not involve a search for the questions for which Sammy found answers. The teacher's plan was for the children to develop their work about animals in a personal direction and to make use of the Internet as the main source of information. One of the aims was to try and use skills from numeracy lessons in the process of answering questions, but the precise skills were not planned for and the direction taken by Sammy, for example, was very different to the directions taken by others in the class. Some of the other areas for investigation included: migration, number of young born and survived, comparative weights of animals (pigs in fact) and humans, and the amount of food eaten per day by different family pets.

This example of Internet-dependent work began as questions to answer and was developed into a self-planned investigation.

There are innumerable sites that provide statistical information. Almost any keyword search linked with the word 'statistics' will yield a large number of websites, many of which will provide suitable numerical information to assist in the collection of data or the solution of problems.

For example, a search using the keywords 'dog' and 'statistics' will lead to sites with serious information about dog breeds and numbers:

(1) http://www.dogsworldwide.com/ where it is possible to search for breed details and statistics.

(2) http://www.thepetprofessor.com/secFunStuff/dog_statistics.html where it is possible to look up facts and figures concerning not only dogs, but all types of pets.

(3) www.hot-dog.org which is the website of the National Hot Dog And Sausage Council and where it tells us such items of hotdog fact as: 'Every summer Americans eat seven billion hotdogs; laid end to end they would reach from New York to Frankfurt in Germany 171 times.' There are many more 'trivia statistics' which can be appealing to some children and can be used to lead into some interesting and useful work. There are also recipes which can inspire and amuse and lead to investigations with the numbers involved.

A search using the phrase 'snoring statistics', though perhaps undertaken light-heartedly, gives access to some facts and figures that are actually not amusing at all.

Two other examples, chosen almost at random from the wealth of numerical riches available, of sites with facts and figures likely to be usable in the context of the primary curriculum are:

www.Adherents.com

This is a collection of over '41,000 adherent statistics and religious geography citations.' It provides details of and detailed statistics for over 4,200 religions, churches, denominations, religious bodies, faith groups, tribes, cultures and movements.

http://www.sunblock99.org.uk/sb99/fact/fact_f.html

Here we are given a range of figures concerning the sun and the solar system. One comment which caught the imagination of a group of nine-year-olds was to the effect that: 'The Sun is a pretty ordinary, five billion year old star!' This short sentence raised many questions concerning both the existence of other ordinary stars, and how many of them there are, and also the notion that any particular entity could actually be five billion years old and what it would mean in terms of the human lifespan.

These two last examples are not included as the best of what the Internet has to offer, but as an illustration that the Internet does have so much to offer. As one Internet enthusiast reported, 'It's all out there, information on absolutely everything – it's just a question of finding it.'

CHAPTER 5

Using other resources from the Internet

At the start of Chapters Three and Four, brief discourses on the value of first 'words', and secondly 'numbers' from the Internet were given. The value of resources other than words and numbers cannot be underestimated. Whether we look at dynamic sites that give insight into scientific principles or processes, sites that give a window into the lives of people in distant regions, or sites designed with other specific educational goals, the value is clear and unmistakable. The positive features of Internet use, of motivation, cultural suitability and social interaction, remain the same, and the nature of these 'different' sites adds to their value in the encouragement of effective learning.

Amongst the many dedicated sites providing resources for education there is much variability. Teachers do not rate very highly the sites that simply present pages of books with an icon which effectively turns the page, or which present on screen other information in a similarly mundane fashion. These sites do not exploit the features of web-based functionality – responding to the user's actions, using speech, linking to other supporting pages or documents, giving access to diagrams or further related information, video clips, linking to other related sites. Conversely, there are a great number of sites that teachers do rate highly and have won awards from various bodies for their excellence in the field. It is these sites which we should be looking towards to integrate into teaching, and possibly for inspiration in our own preparation for web-based, or Internet reliant, teaching. In this chapter we will look at some of the ways in which children can be encouraged to engage in tasks that make use of some of the dynamic and interactive sites on the Internet, in order to further their learning and their enjoyment of learning.

Scientific investigation and exploration can benefit from the use of dynamic and sometimes interactive media. Some websites simply demonstrate a scientific principle, or show a simple mechanism in action and in doing so give a greater insight into the principles and processes involved than a two-dimensional diagram could ever hope to give. Access to such sites can make the difference between understanding and not understanding the process in question. There are many CD-ROM-based programs which include interactivity and dynamic features, but to search out the best and then to spend money on them when a freely accessible option exists is not always the best way forward. Time does need to be spent in searching out appropriate sites, but through the gateway of the National Grid for Learning and other well-known and reputable sites, it is not always too difficult a task for the busy teacher.

Moving Diagrams

One such example came to light when a search was undertaken for examples of cams. A cam is a feature of a variety of mechanisms and cams are often used by children in the course of work in Design and Technology. The best way to explore the notion of a cam is probably to examine toys, or other mechanical devices which actually make use of cams in the way that they work. The second best way to learn about cams is, possibly, to watch an animated cam in action. Such an animation was found: www.dtonline.org. The site was in fact not a dazzling all-action version of what might have been found. It was actually a very low-key site but with excellent moving representations of gears, cams, levers, pulleys and linkages. With the use of a large screen, the class were shown the essential aspects of cams along with other interesting and arresting moving representations of other mechanical devices. The work proceeded well, and the temptation for some children to visit the site and relive the wonder which they derived from the moving images was hard to overcome. One child in particular spent an inordinate length of time watching and re-watching the movement of the cam in the animation.

It is worth considering here the progress of the search for moving images of cams, since we have not looked in any detail at the problems which can be faced when undertaking searches on the Internet.

The progress made through the search is interesting because it illustrates a principle which is often found useful. The principle is: carry out a broad search with perhaps one keyword ('cam' in this example); progressively narrow down the search by adding further keywords or phrases (levers, pulleys, linkages, and finally the phrase 'design and technology'). Different search engines set out the procedure for searching differently. Google, finally used in the example below, gives a 'Search within results' option which allows a further search on the restricted, though at times very large, set of sites that were discovered in the initial search. It is worth reading the 'Tips for searching' information when using a search engine for the first time, as the ways and means of carrying out certain types of searches can be different.

The teacher involved in this work, and who carried out the searches, was able to make a comparison with the same work – making a simple toy involving a cam, which she had undertaken the previous year. Although she did not evaluate it

Table 5.1 Cam search chart

Starting point/search	Result/Comment
Learning Alive home page www.learningalive.co.uk/	Learning Alive is a site used by many schools as a 'gateway' to the Internet. It has access to search facilities and a host of other school-centred features. For many of the features there is a subscription charge.
↓ Search the Internet	
↓ Yahoo Search Engine Keyword search 'cam'	About 17,000,000 websites found. Since the word 'cam' in Internet parlance refers to a web camera these results were of no use. Those not relating to a camera seemed to relate to 'computer assisted manufacture'.
↓ Yahoo Search Engine Advanced search Keywords 'cam' and 'mechanics'	90,000 websites. Most seemed to be related to CAD/CAM (Computer Assisted Design/Computer Assisted Manufacture) and car engines.
↓ Yahoo Search Engine Advanced search Keywords 'cam' and 'machine'	404,000 websites, none of which seemed to be appropriate.
↓ Change of search engine: Google Keywords 'cams levers pulleys linkages'	238 sites found.
↓ Add the phrase 'design and technology' to the keywords	68 sites returned. Most seem to relate to GCSE syllabuses.
↓ Try a promising site further down the list: **www.dtonline.org**	Choice of different topics to look at.
↓ Choose 'mechanisms' and then 'information' and then 'cams and followers'	Useful diagram of a cam.
↓ Go back and look at 'rotary cams'	Animated diagram of a working rotary cam and a simple explanation. Exactly what was required.
↓ Note the address of the site and save the page as a bookmark/favourite.	

Note: Another site with a moving image was also located at technology student.com/cams/cam1.htm. This site was equally good in its animation, and it gave a lot more background information for the teacher. She chose not to use it because the screen was too 'cluttered with words', which she considered would be a distraction for her children.

ormally, and recognising that a range of variables may well have made an impact on the way that the children worked, and on the end products, she felt that having had access to the animated cam was an important factor in the level of interest taken by a good proportion of the class, and she also felt that in an overall sense, the standard of the work was better than the year before.

Figure 5.1

The Human Body

At the beginning of a science topic in Key Stage Two, focusing on Life Processes and Living Things, and in particular, human movement it was decided that the Internet might provide the impetus for a successful unit of work. The teacher wanted her class to gain more experience of using the Internet and in so doing make progress through the programme of study for ICT, in particular in the strand dealing with 'Finding Things Out'. The teacher considered herself an Internet novice and made the decision to put into practice what she had heard about on courses and from other teachers in the school. From her understanding of the Internet and the pedagogy associated with Internet use, she considered that a search was the most obvious starting point. In the event this did prove to be a successful move, but it is often not the best policy when dealing with inexperienced users, especially if simple searches have not been used previously. The children in the Year 5 class had not been formally taught about searching, indeed they had not had access to the Internet at school at all. About one third of the class had used the Internet at home, but their knowledge of searching and refining searches was limited.

The teacher gave a very brief introduction to the work, which took place in the ICT suite. She introduced them to a search engine, demonstrated a simple search with one keyword – football, and then asked the class to find a website that showed them how skeletons worked. This minimalist introduction was not ideal, but the tenacity of the class and their willingness to work together and share their findings, linked to the motivation and excitement which the use of the Internet generated, proved to be powerful in the children's hands and the results of this one session were, in many ways, remarkable.

Word spread very quickly and everyone had soon located the games that were available. Since the games were well designed and required, in most cases, a good deal of thought, children were involved in a range of play-related learning activities. The teacher commented later that the room buzzed with both excitement and with quality activity. The animations, and the control over the animations, were another extremely popular activities which the children became involved in.

By the end of the lesson the children were able to talk not only about the names and locations of bones, but about the purposes of particular bones, the types of injuries which occur most often in particular bones, the different types of articulating joint, the connections between muscles and bones, and in one case some of the subtle differences between the skeleton of a gorilla and a human, and more commonly the differences between male and female human skeletons. Not all of the children were expert in all of the topics listed above, but they were all covered and considered in the class.

By the end of the lesson it was clear that a good deal of learning had taken place and that it had taken place in an atmosphere of excitement and enjoyment. The motivational powers of both the Internet and the subject matter had combined to provide a context for learning which suited those involved. The high quality of the sites visited and used also had an important role to play in the success of the lesson.

The teacher changed the plans which she had made for the next lesson and decided to capitalise on the resource which she had unexpectedly tapped into. She set a slightly more formal task for the following lesson and the children were given the task of producing a fact sheet entitled 'The Human Skeleton – everything that we should know'. The children worked in pairs and the end products were very good. The practical skill of cutting and pasting pictures from the Internet, something that was a mystery to the teacher, was passed around the room and soon fact sheets including pictures, annotated diagrams and short pieces of text were emerging. The teacher was immensely impressed with the Internet as a resource for this work and had her original, slightly sceptical, view of the Internet reformed.

MEET THE SKELETON FROM THE GRAVE

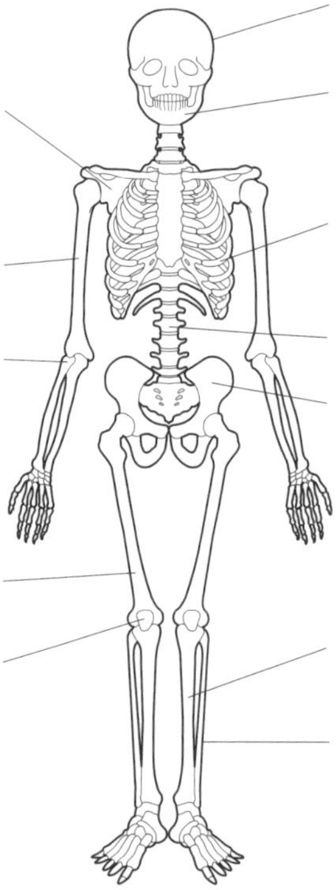

SID THE SKEL

We all have a skeleton, without it we would be a blob of stuff on the ground.

The skeleton keeps you safe, it protects the soft things in your body like the brain and your lungs.

The biggest bone is in your legs called the femur

Here are the names.
Can you label **Sid the Skel.**
Femur
Patella
Ulna
Radius
Vertebra
Ribs
Skull
Tibia
Fibula
Humerus
Jaw
Pelvis

Figure 5.2 *One child's fact sheet*

Of the many sites visited on that first afternoon, those below proved to be the most engaging for the children, and are worthy of note here.

The MadSci network www.madsci.org/

This site, which emanates from a seemingly private operation in Boston, USA, is billed as the laboratory that never sleeps. It contains good quality explanations of scientific ideas and, amongst many other areas of work, an option to 'Ask a Scientist'. The MadSci site also has many links to other more specialist sites, for example, the Visible Human Body.

e-skeletons www.eskeletons.org/

This is the site which gives access to views of bones, from many different orientations and allows for comparisons between humans, gorillas and baboons. The views of teeth are particularly clear and interesting. There are also animations of moving bones and joints. The site is owned and maintained by an educational institution in Texas, USA.

Medtropolis www.medtropolis.com/VBody.asp

Again based in the USA and aiming to 'educate and entertain adults and kids alike', which it certainly did in the case in point. Most educational and entertaining was the 'Build a Skeleton' game, which includes an optional narration that can be very useful for certain children. The feature that allows for 'organising your organs', though not strictly on the topic of the skeleton, proved to be particularly captivating.

Innerbody www.innerbody.com/htm/body.html

There are a great many simple diagrams accompanied by text to explain what is in the diagrams. The particular point of interest here, which was not found anywhere else, was the section that illustrated broken bones. The explanation of the hip replacement operation, in full diagrammatic glory, attracted the attention of one child who was able to talk at length about the process and relate it to his Grandad who was, at that time, recovering from the operation. The ability to identify closely with the operation and being able to share his close family experience was an important factor in the success of the work. The child's involvement and interest spilled over to much of the rest of the class. They were well motivated to begin with anyway, because of the novel and dynamic nature of the sites which they were visiting.

Innerbody seems to be the educational wing of the a company called Intellimed and has a vision 'To provide high-quality educational content through low-bandwidth Internet access to children, parents and schools worldwide,' which it certainly seems to be fulfilling.

BBC Science www.bbc.co.uk/science/humanbody/

This site provides a range of excellent animations controlled by the user, and a game which requires a good deal of thought. This site is of the same high quality that the BBC has provided for schools over many years now. This site is not actually a part of the BBC Schools set-up, but that is no reason for it not being used by schools.

All of the sites that were used in the lesson and are listed above were active and accessible at the time of writing, which is helpful, but websites do come and go for a variety of reasons and it is important to check that a site still exists in the form that you last saw it if you intend to base any work around the site.

Exploring Pond Life

As a part of work in Key Stage One (Humans and other animals; Living things in their environments) the Nature Grid website (www.naturegrid.org.uk/pond

explorer/key.html) proved a good resource in the identification of creatures found in a school pond. There are many good, child-centred identification keys and charts available from a variety of sources – books and posters for example, but the moving images available through this site add a dimension which is not available through other easily accessible means.

The site proved to be the only resource, apart from a real pond in the school grounds, used by the teacher, although plans had been made to use a range of topic books from the School Library Service. The fact that the books arrived too late to be useful did not, in the event, present a problem.

The Nature Grid site, which is managed by the Canterbury Environmental Education Centre, is a collection of activities and information presented in a range of different forms. It is extremely easy to use the site and has an impressive range of resources for teachers as well as for children. The Pond Explorer is made up of six areas:

- Teachers' Notes – comprehensive advice and a number of links to other sites relevant to the topic and of use to teachers.
- Virtual Pond Dip – very clear images of pond creatures photographed in a large white container. Each tiny creature is hyperlinked to a larger diagram on an information page.
- Exploring Pond Habitats – a straightforward cross-sectional view of a typical pond with links from each area, which explains the differences between one part of the pond and another and the reasons why different creatures are found in different parts of the whole environment.
- Pond Investigation – a step-by-step guide to using a pond as a resource. The main part of this site is for children, and explains how to approach a pond dipping session, the teachers' notes give a session by session guide to a topic relating to ponds, creatures and pond environments. Safety considerations are included and reference to the ways in which visits to the Canterbury Environmental Centre are conducted. The fact that one particular environmental centre was featured on the site, and that visits to the site are available for schools was not a stumbling block to the use of the site – the school, in the Midlands, was far too distant to contemplate a visit. Other centres exist which can be visited, but in this case the school pond and environmental area, fenced off in the corner of the field served as the essential first-hand element of the work.
- Activity Sheets – simple printable sheets in the form of a 'Passport to Ponds' are included and can be used or added to as suits the needs of the teacher and children at the time.
- Identification Key – probably the most impressive aspect of the site, and certainly of most interest to the children who spent good quality time with their

collection of pond creatures and a magnifying class sifting through the pictures, diagrams and moving images in their efforts to identify precisely what is was that they had collected.

The Nature Grid site includes many other unusual resources apart from the Pond Explorer. For example, there is an area dealing with recycling: www.naturegrid.org.uk/eco-exp/games.html#bottle; an area looking at the production of a nature-based sculpture: www.naturegrid.org.uk/expart/whprcss.html; and a section entitled 'I didn't know I ate that', which is presented as a very simple interactive game, and introduces information about what it is that we actually eat, in terms of seed, roots, flowers, stems and fruit: www.naturegrid.org.uk/plant/foodparts.html and is linked to another set of pages which help children to investigate more about the types of food which we eat: www.naturegrid.org.uk/plant/foodplant1.html#top.

Primary Sources in History

www.j-sainsbury.co.uk/museum/museum.htm

There are many sites, including those linked to museums, both real and virtual, which are repositories for historical documents and artefacts. Amongst these documents are gems of historical interest waiting to be used by those who, under other circumstances might not find too much of interest in history. Among the archive materials are documents of all kinds, pictures and posters, some audio recordings of famous speeches from important points in our history and also collections of film footage.

The Sainsbury's museum contains all of the above mentioned categories of historical source, much of it in quantity, and it is certainly of very good quality. All of the resources relate in some way or another to the development of the giant supermarkets which most of us are familiar with today. Certain sections of the virtual museum relate to times and events in the history of Britain, which impacted on the running of large retail outlets – for example, World War Two.

The museum is set out in the form of a large building with different rooms housing different parts of the museum. The rooms include:

- A cinema, where there are a selection of video clips, most of which are reasonably short, less than one minute in most cases. The clips are taken from a 1960s promotional film showing a range of scenes, with soundtracks, from around a typical store of the time; each 1960s clip is matched with a similar situation filmed in 2002. The comparisons are very interesting and can be a stimulus for understanding the process of change that takes place over time. There are also a range of audio files that give an insight into other aspects of the social history of shops and shopping.

- A shop, where images of food packets and containers are displayed and available for copying and printing.
- A case study of the East Grinstead store, which gives an account of the store's existence through the difficult times of World War Two.
- World War Two. It is this section, with links to some of the other sections too, which contains the most remarkable documents in the museum. One part of this exhibition contains the many memoranda sent from head office to store managers concerning the employment of women during the war. This was obviously a difficult topic for the managers to deal with, and plenty of advice about how and where to make use of female staff members is given. For example, there is a list of departments where women may and may not be deployed. There are suggestions that the women may not have well-developed arithmetic skills; warnings about familiarity, and many more topics which were of major concern at the time, but would be considered somewhat out of place now.
- People at Sainsbury's contains detail of different individuals' work patterns and rates of pay. Insight into the life of unknown workers can often inspire the interest of children when the lives of the great and the good fail to do so. Children in many cases are able to identify with the ordinary people more easily than with famous names.

There is also a Schools' gallery which exhibits project work submitted by schools and is rotated on a regular basis.

There are reference sections for teachers. Provision is made for teachers at all four Key Stages, and there is certainly scope for developing both content-based work from the primary Key Stages, and historical skills, since the provision of detailed pictures of the time, and a range of written documents and posters and adverts, supply a rich history of the company through many years. The earliest documents and pictures date back to the 1850s. There is a Bureau de Change which allows for imperial weights and measures, as well as £sd currency to be worked with and converted to the units more easily understood by children today.

Children, in many cases, are able to explore the site unaided. Indeed teachers have on occasion put their plans to one side for a while and allowed free exploration of what is a very captivating site. The Sainsbury's Museum is approved and recommended by both the National Grid for Learning, and the Virtual Teacher Centre.

Life in the Mease Valley

http://www.maryhoward.staffs.sch.uk/resource/

Geography at Key Stage One has a requirement under the Breadth of Study heading that children should make a study of their local area. This is often a straightforward opportunity for teachers to plan and deliver. However for Key

Stage Two, the study is to be of another locality in the British isles, as well as localities in other countries. This is less straightforward to organise in many cases. Ideally a visit to a contrasting location might be organised. For some schools this is possible and is given priority. In many other schools, for a variety of reasons, including cost, it is not possible to visit a location for the purposes of study, and alternative approaches are used.

One such approach to the study of a contrasting location was taken by a school in a deprived area of a large city. Many of the children had not visited other areas of the country and even fewer had travelled abroad. The approach taken involved making use of a website created by two schools in rural Staffordshire.

The site, which was clearly put together with care, is made up of a series of screens with links to other sections dealing with many aspects of country life. It is jointly managed by the two schools, one in each of the two villages featured in the tour of the locality.

The topics covered are:

(1) The History of Clifton

(2) The History of Edingale

(3) Landscape and Farming

(4) Houses

(5) Amenities

(6) Children from Clifton say . . .

(7) Children from Edingale say . . .

At the time of using the site the last two sections offering the thoughts of children from the schools had not been completed. It is not entirely clear what will feature on these pages, but the opportunity for web publishing here is obvious. It would also be a useful and possibly fruitful additional feature if the opportunity to comment and ask questions could be added. Indeed, this may well be a part of the planning for development of the site.

The work in the inner-city school focused on farming, and the links to the Landscape and Farming pages were a good introduction to a way of life quite alien to the children involved. The farming-based topic progressed well and included a look at various aspects of farming suggested by the information on the site. The class of children were able to spend a day at the National Agricultural Centre's Children's Farm and have some first-hand experience of a little of what had been encountered through the medium of the Mease Valley website.

The teacher, who had not encountered the Mease Valley prior to this work, exploited other Internet resources in the planning of the topic. In order to give more detail to the study of a contrasting locality, a search was undertaken and a total of sixty-four 'Mease Valley' sites were found. Some of the most useful were supported by the Diocese of Lichfield, and were made up of detail about and pictures of the churches of the parishes in the Mease Valley. There was also a good deal of information relating to the early history of the area, the Roman occupation of the area and also of the time of the Anglo-Saxons. There were also other contrasting sites found: one relating to a luxury country hotel with views over the valley, and an extract from Hansard with the detail of a written answer given in the House of Commons referring to comparative levels of deprivation in the Mease Valley and surrounding areas. Overall, considering the nature of the area and its lack of a national profile generally, there was much to be found and used.

A Virtual Tour of a Gurdwara

www.thegrid.org.uk/learning/re/pupil/sikh/index.html

In contrast to the examples above, a virtual tour of the Watford Sikh Gurdwara provides access to and insight into a religion and a religious building which might not otherwise be possible. Schools in some areas do have opportunities to visit churches and temples, and this is always a valuable experience. In areas where this is not possible, a virtual, and very well-organised, tour is a good substitute. The virtual tour can also be used as an introductory activity to a real tour.

At each stage of the tour the children were introduced to practical considerations, the size of the kitchen, storage space for shoes, some of which raised questions about the procedures for worship. The tour was accompanied by short descriptions which more or less named the parts of the building or the particular item or artefact being looked at. There are also questions posed that the children were asked to speculate about. The style of the questions is good, because they did not expect correct answers in many cases, and they encouraged the children to make suggestions based upon what they could see and the small amount of information given. Elsewhere on the site is a link to a BBC archive where there is a talk given during Lent 2002 by a Sikh academic. As a novel source of information this was extremely well received. Having control over the recording proved to be a useful tool. The teacher was able to stop and draw attention to particular sections of the talk, and also to replay certain sections which needed explanation. The text of the talk was also available on the website (www.bbc.co.uk/religion/programmes/lent_talks/scripts/khalidi.html) and sections of this were used to help the class come to understand what they had listened to. The higher ability group in the class were given a section of the text from which they produced a summary, using skills of extracting main ideas from text which they had been working on in their literacy lessons. They shared their summaries with the rest of the class in a plenary feedback session. Some of the talk included quotations from Sikh holy writing; this was looked at (in English script) and the teacher was able to provide translations garnered from another, non-web-based, resource.

In this example the class were not able to visit a gurdwara, but given the detail and interest generated by the virtual tour, this short part of a project looking at Places of Worship was evaluated as having been successful. Judging from the apparent knowledge of the children when later questioned about different places of worship, it seemed that the work concerning the gurdwara, by means of this website, had made the most impact. The teacher was keen to replicate this experience with other religious buildings, but no similar sites could be found at the time or in the time available. A virtual tour of the holy city of Jerusalem was available, (www.md.huji.ac.il/vjt/) but could not really be justified for inclusion in the short RE topic looking at worship in the UK. The children did make real visits to other religious buildings which were accessible in the area.

Webquests

The notion of a Webquest comes from the United States. A Webquest can be as small or as large as suits its creator and consists of an introductory web page which sets out both content and activity. That is, children are set to work on a particular project, given information, tasks and links to further supporting information and expected, with appropriate teacher support, to fulfil what is asked of them. Webquests vary greatly in their style and intentions, some are expansive and designed to provide the backbone of the work in a particular topic for a whole school term; others are less grand and serve to introduce a topic, to reinforce other activities or to act as a conclusion to work carried out.

Webquests are built loosely around a central structure that consists of a series of headings and for each heading there is an expectation that certain information will be given and that certain tasks and related learning activities will be set out to be completed by the children following the quest. The Webquest UK site tells us that:

> All Webquests follow a clearly defined structure. Some uses of the internet stop at the point where pupils locate web resources. Webquests require pupils to reconstruct their learning into a report or presentation of their own. (Webquest UK, undated)

The underpinning theory is apparently close to some of the ideas that were considered in Chapter Two, and for that reason it is worth looking at the whole area of Webquests. It must be noted that Webquests are actually quite variable. There is no fixed and inflexible approach which must be taken, and there are not rules for their creation which are set in concrete. There is, however, a structure that all Webquests follow. The structure is not a straitjacket; there is scope for developing activities in many of the ways that have been described earlier in this book. If account is taken of the context of the work, attention is given to pre-existing knowledge, and the social constructivist notions of collaboration and co-operation are put into practice, the power of the Webquest to promote enjoyable and effective learning can be great.

The headings in the Webquest structure are:

- A title – the name of the Webquest. This can be something designed to inspire interest, or a simple description of the content of the quest.
- An introduction – this is often short and sets the scene for what is to come.
- Process – what to do. This section sets out the task or tasks that are to be completed. Often a good deal of guidance is given and suggestions for how to complete the tasks.
- Resources – this section can vary enormously. There can be documents, diagrams, photographs, maps, sound files, video clips and access to primary sources. In short, anything that will be needed to complete the tasks. In most cases the resources are embedded within the structure of the Webquest, but there are also opportunities for links to be made to other locations on the Internet where access can be made to sources of information needed to complete the tasks.
- Evaluation – in this section the success criteria are made very clear to the children. They are told what it is that they have to do in order to have completed the quest successfully.

The idea of making learning objectives clear at the start of a lesson is becoming common in many schools. If children are clear about what is expected of them it is far more likely that they will be able to achieve it. In many classrooms throughout the country teachers write a learning objective on the board at the beginning of lessons and draw it to the attention of the class. In this way, it is thought, children are able to understand what it is they are doing and to what end. It seems to be a successful approach.

The Ozline website sets out the features of a Webquest that are required to be in place if it is to considered, formally, to be a Webquest, and if it is likely to be successful in its aims. It is reproduced opposite as Table 5.2.

Bernie Dodge, the creator of Webquests, has written widely on the subject and has provided many examples, both of his own, and of others, on the main Webquest site, in the USA (webquest.sdsu.edu/). Examples of Webquests set in the context of the UK National Curriculum, and many that are based upon the schemes of work produced by the QCA are found via the Webquest UK site (www.webquestuk.org.uk/).

An article by Bernie Dodge that sets out the philosophy and implementation of Webquests is a good starting point for those who would like to know more (Dodge 1997).

Naturally, it would be possible to create a Webquest with little or no attention

Table 5.2 Features of a Webquest

Engaging Opening	Has that 'something' that compels attention.
The Question/Task	Clear Question and Task. These naturally flow from the introduction and signal a direction for learning.
Background for Everyone	Clearly calls attention to the need for a common foundation of knowledge and provides needed resources.
Roles/Expertise	Roles match the issues and resources. The roles provide multiple perspectives from which to view the topic.
Use of the Web	Uses the Web to access at least some of the following: interactivity, multiple perspectives, current information.
Transformative Thinking	Higher level thinking required to construct new meaning. Scaffolding is clearly provided to support student achievement.
Real World Feedback	Some feedback loop is included in the Web page. May include a rubric for success.
Conclusion	Clear tie-in to the intro. Makes the students' cognitive tasks overt and suggests how this learning could transfer to other domains/issues.

to encouraging constructivist learning. Tasks could be set which require little engagement, thought or collaboration. For this reason it would be wrong to say that all Webquests are good. Each example needs to be considered and used or not used according to what is found. When teachers produce Webquests for their own use they are tailored exactly to the needs that the teacher has identified. In these cases there will be a good contextual match with the setting of the school and the background of the children; the previous experience of the class will be taken into account as will the range of abilities and the particular needs of small groups or individual children. In short, Webquests can be a very good resource; those created by others can be good, but those created 'in-house' are most often better. Once the initial work has been undertaken, a Webquest can be used many times, perhaps with a little modification from time to time.

An example will serve to illustrate. It will always be problematic in a context such as this book, to give a web address and expect it to last for evermore. Some excellent sites simply disappear overnight with little or no explanation. However, the sites referred to here were up and running smoothly at the time of writing and should they have disappeared by the time of reading, a keyword search for 'webquest' will give access to many other examples.

The Greek Worship Webquest is simple and straightforward for children to use. There is a teachers' section which provides copies of the sheets mentioned and other advice about using it.

The opening paragraphs from the teachers' page give a clear picture of the way that the Webquest links to the National Curriculum for History, and the way in which the quest has been planned and should be used: 'These pages make up a web enquiry designed for Year 5 children studying the QCA History Unit 14

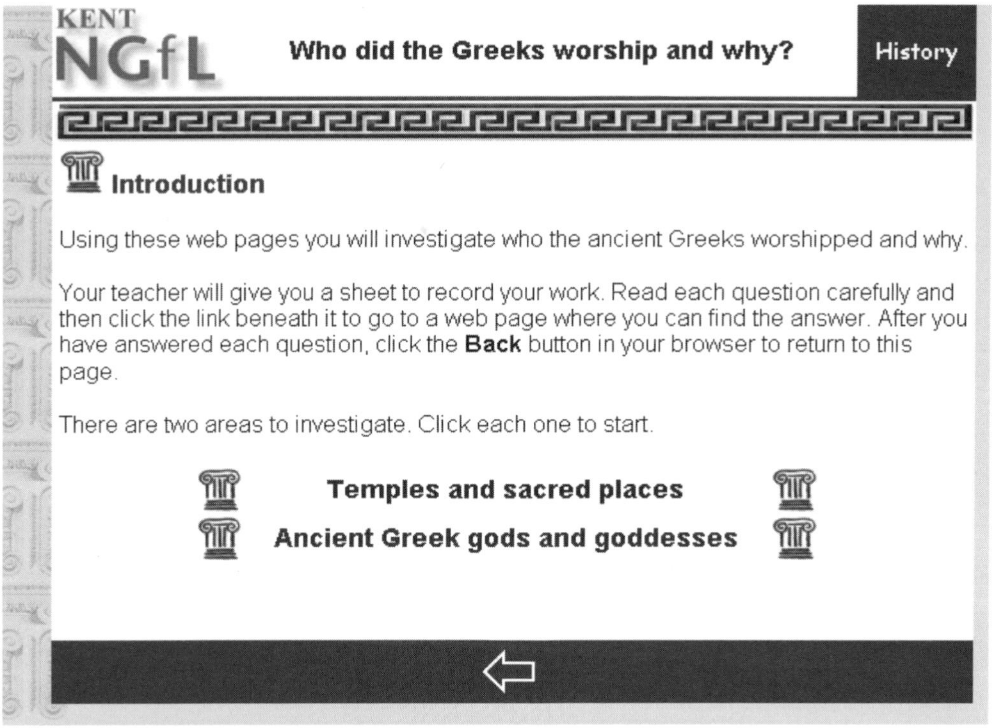
KENT
NGfL
Who did the Greeks worship and why?
History
Introduction
Using these web pages you will investigate who the ancient Greeks worshipped and why.
Your teacher will give you a sheet to record your work. Read each question carefully and then click the link beneath it to go to a web page where you can find the answer. After you have answered each question, click the Back button in your browser to return to this page.
There are two areas to investigate. Click each one to start.
Temples and sacred places
Ancient Greek gods and goddesses

www.kented.org.uk/ngfl/webenquiry/greeks/

Figure 5.3 Opening page of a Webquest about Greek Worship

"Who were the ancient Greeks?". The activities centre around ancient Greek religion and help the children investigate who the ancient Greeks worshipped and why.'

The Greek Worship Webquest is an example of what Dodge (1997) has termed a short-term Webquest, it is designed to be completed in a relatively short space of time, probably no more than two or three lessons. Other Webquests are designed to last for longer periods.

A series of questions is presented on a web page. After each question is a link to a web resource where the children will find information that will help them reach an answer.

Not all the answers are directly contained in the resources, the children should be encouraged to infer answers from the historical sources presented. Some questions ask the children for their opinions and an explanation.

There are two sheets to help the children record their findings. They are in Microsoft Word format and can be printed and given to the children before they begin the enquiry. The teachers' page is found at:
http://www.kented.org.uk/ngfl/weben quiry/greeks/ teacher.html.

A list of other interesting Webquests, and related sites is included at the end of this chapter, it is by no means exhaustive, simply illustrative.

There is a Webquest about creating Webquests, just a little esoteric, which can be found at: http://www.otterbein.edu/dept/educ/sciquests/worksheet.html. There are also, available through Webquest sites, templates which can be used to make the creation of a new Webquest as straightforward as possible.

It would be possible to include a good deal more here concerning the background, practice and theory of Webquests, but it is not wholly appropriate. There is as much information, and many links, to be found at the Webquest UK website: www.webquestuk.org.uk

The examples given in this chapter of the ways in which resources from the Internet which are not wholly words, or wholly numbers, only give a small hint of the possibilities which exist for developing tasks and activities designed to capture children's interest and enhance the learning opportunities which teachers provide. The same can be said for the examples given in earlier chapters too, relating to other resources used to enhance the learning experiences of children. Most of the Internet is not primarily aimed at an educational market, but a good proportion of what exists, whether aimed at schools or not, has the potential for use in well-structured programmes devised by teachers in order to generate enthusiasm and engagement in topics being studied. To look at the examples in this book as the only uses to which the Internet might be put would be to limit the vast scope which is offered by the ever growing worldwide encyclopaedia which is the Internet. The Internet is an encyclopaedia, but it is much, much more besides. It is a highly valuable and incomparable resource for almost all of the activities which are undertaken both within schools and without, for the purpose of enjoyment and learning.

Examples of Sites with Novel Approaches and Interesting, Useful Content

In this last section a range of current websites is listed. These sites are further examples of more unusual sites which offer opportunities to teachers and children to develop work in ways other than reading or 'being told'. The sites here offer a range of opportunities for constructive, collaborative and interactive learning which encourage engagement with facts and ideas. They are most certainly not the only sites which offer these opportunities; there are many more which teachers are finding and exploiting on a regular basis, to the all-round benefit of their pupils and their own professional development. A selection of freely accessible Webquests are also included. Again, this is not because they are the best available, but because they illustrate the range of possibilities offered by the medium.

Science-Based

Neuroscience for kids:
faculty.washington.edu/chudler/neurok.html

Control of a very powerful microscope:
micro.magnet.fsu.edu/primer/java/electronmicroscopy/magnify1/index.html

Space exploration:
amazing-space.stsci.edu/
Recycling game and associated activities:
www.epa.gov/recyclecity/gameitro. htm
Information and activity for Key Stage One based around tomatoes:
www.thetomatozone.co.uk/#
Very large distances – from deep space to the structure of DNA:
micro. magnet.fsu.edu/primer/java/scienceopticsu/powersof10/index.html

Beginning with a view of the solar system from the outside, the above site leads us to a view of Earth from a distance of millions of light years away to 10 attometers which is very small indeed. It comes to a halt with a view beyond of strands of DNA to the smallest element of an object that it is currently possible to define.

Live weather data
www.napier.demon.co.uk/weather/station.html
www-atm.physics.ox.ac.uk/weather/
www.wunderground.com/global/AU_QU.html
UK Met Office:
www.metoffice.com/
Education:
www.metoffice.com/education/index.html
Animated charts:
www.metoffice.com/weather/charts/animation.html

Other Topics

The meaning of life:
www.pcfre.org.uk/db/
Music Games:
www.bbc.co.uk/radio3/games/index.shtml
Quiz Maker:
www.mape.org.uk/kids/index.htm This is to be found at the Micros and Primary Education (MAPE) site (www.mape.org.uk/), along with a range of resources for teachers.
Whodunnit? (Playing Detective). Also found at the MAPE site.

Webquests and Related Sites

Ancient Egypt Webquest:
www.iwebquest.com/egypt/ancientegypt.htm
Noah's Ark Webquest:
www.webquestuk.org.uk/Completed%20Quests/Noah%27s% 20Ark/Index.htm
Victorian Britain:
www.kented.org.uk/ngfl/webenquiry/victorians/

A Rainforest Webquest:

http://www.webquestuk.org.uk/Completed%20Quests/Junior%20Rainforest/rain.htm

Hippopotamus Webquest:

http://www.berksiu.k12.pa.us/webquest/Wadsworth/ Index.htm

Webquest dealing with a wide range of 'amazing' animals:

http://www. berksiu. k12.pa.us/webquest/Campbell/index.htm

Problem-solving in the context of running a Pet Shop:

http://www.geocities. com/mrsevon/webquest.html

Catalogue of example sites, some are at secondary level, but there are some very interesting examples:

http://www-sci.lib.uci.edu/SEP/CTS98/

Another large, searchable catalogue of Webquests, mostly from the USA, but again with some very good examples:

http://its.guilford.k12.nc.us/webquests/ index.htm

UK Webquest site:

www.webquestuk.org.uk/

Webquest Generator:

www.teach-nology.com/web_tools/web_quest/

References and bibliography

Bartlett, F.C. (1932) *Remembering: An Experimental and Social Study* Cambridge University Press: Cambridge.

Bartlett, F.C. (1958) *Thinking* Basic Books: New York.

Becker, H. (2000) Pedagogical motivations for pupil computer use that lead to student engagement. *Educational Technology* **40** (5), 5–17.

Bereiter, C. and Scardamalia, M. (1987) *The Psychology of Written Composition* Laurence Erlbaum Associates: Hillsdale NJ.

Brown, A. (1987) Metacognition, executive control, self-regulation, and other more mysterious mechanisms. *In* F. E. Weinert and R. H. Kluwe (eds) *Metacognition, Motivation, and Understanding* Lawrence Erlbaum Associates: Hillsdale, New Jersey, 65–116.

Brown, J. S., Collins, A. and Duigud, P. (1989) Situated cognition and the culture of learning. *Educational Researcher* **18** (1) 32–42.

Bruner, J. (1996) *The Culture of Education* Harvard University Press: Cambridge MA.

Chandler, D. (1984) *Young Learners and the Microcomputer* Open University Press: Milton Keynes.

Cox, M.J. (1997) The effects of Information Technology on students' motivation: final report. NCET.

Davis, P. M. (1991). *Cognition and Learning: A Review of the Literature with Reference to Ethnolinguistic Minorities* Dallas, TX: Summer Institute of Linguistics.

DfES (2002) *Annual Survey of Information and Communications Technology in Schools* London.

DfEE (1999) *Superhighway Safety, Children's Safe Use of the Internet* London.

DfEE/QCA (1999a) *The National Curriculum: Handbook for Primary Teachers in England* DfEE/QCA: London.

DfEE/QCA (1999b) *National Numeracy Strategy* DfEE/QCA: London.

Dodge, B. (1997) Some thoughts about WebQuests edweb.sdsu.edu/courses/edtec596/about_webquests.html (Accessed 14.02.04).

Flavell, J. H. (1976) Metacognitive aspects of problem solving. In Resnick (ed.) *The Nature of Intelligence* Lawrence Erlbaum Associates: New Jersey, 231–235.

Flavell, J. H. (1977) *Cognitive Development* Prentice-Hall: Englewood Cliffs, New Jersey.

Gardner, H. (1993) *Multiple Intelligences: The Theory in Practice* Basic Books: New York.

Gardner, H. (1983) *Frames of Mind* Basic Books: New York.

Harris, S. and Kington, A. (2002) Innovative classroom practice using ICT in England: the second information technology in education study (SITES) www.nfer.ac.uk/research/down_pub.asp (Accessed 14.02.04).

Hennessy, S. (2000) Graphing investigations using portable (palmtop) technology. *Journal of Computer Assisted Learning,* **16**, 243–258.

Heppell, S. (2003) Contribution to the Information Technology and Teacher Education (ITTE) mail list on the tread of the difference between IT and ICT.

Holbrook, H. (1984). ERIC/RCS: Pre-reading in the content areas. *Journal of Reading,* **27**, 368–370.

Holland, J.H., Holyoak, K.J., Nisbett, R.E. and Thagard, P.R. (1986) *Induction: Processes of Inference, Learning and Discovery* MIT Press: Cambridge MA.

ImaCT2 (2001) *The Impact of Information and Communication Technologies on Pupil Learning and Attainment* BECTa Found at: www.becta.org.uk/research/research.cfm?section=1&id=539 (Accessed 14.02.04).

Ipgrave, J. (2002) *Pupil to Pupil Dialogue in the Classroom as a Tool for Religious Education* (Warwick Religious and Education Research Unit Occasional Paper 2) Warwick Institute of Education, University of Warwick.

Jonassen, David H. *et al,* (1999) *Learning With Technology: A Constructivist Perspective* Columbus, Ohio: Merrill/Prentice-Hall.

Johnson-Laird, P. (1983) *Mental Models: Towards a Cognitive Science of Language, Inference, and Consciousness* Harvard University Press, Cambridge MA.

Kolb, D. (1984) *Experiential Learning: Experience as the Source of Learning and Development* Prentice-Hall, Inc.: Englewood Cliffs, N.J.

Lave, J. and Wenger, E. (1991) *Situated Learning* Cambridge University Press, Cambridge.

Lewis, M., Wray, D. and Rospigliosi, P. (1995) 'No copying please': helping children respond to non-fiction text. *Education 3-13,* **23** 1.

McFarlane, A. (ed.) (1997) *Information Technology and Authentic Learning: Realising the Potential of Computers in the Primary Classroom* Routledge: London.

Marland, M. (1981) *Information Skills in the Secondary Curriculum* Methuen, London.

Moseley, D. and Higgins, S. (1999) *Ways Forward with ICT: Effective Pedagogy using Information and Communications Technology for Literacy and Numeracy in Primary Schools.* www.ncl.ac.uk/ecls/research/project_ttaict/TTA_ICT.pdf (Accessed 14.02.04) University of Newcastle/TTA.

NCET (1995) *Making Sense of Information* NCET Coventry.

NCET (1997) *Primary Mathematics with IT* NCET Coventry.

Ozline (2003) Assessing WebQuests www.ozline.com/webquests/rubric.html (Accessed 14.02.04).

Papert, S. (1982) *Mindstorms: Children Computers and Powerful Ideas* The Harvester Press: Brighton.

Pachler, N. and Williams, L. (1999) *Using the Internet as Teaching and Learning Tool* in Leask, M. and Pachler, N. (1999) *Learning to Teach Using ICT in the Secondary School* Routledge Falmer: London.

Posner, M. (ed.) *Foundations of Cognitive Science* MIT Press: Cambridge MA.

Pritchard, A (1997) Logo, motivation, and a project about garden gates in a primary classroom. *British Journal of Educational Technology* **28**, no. 1, 5–18.

Pritchard, A. and Cartwright, V. (2004) Transforming what they read: helping eleven year olds engage with Internet Information *Literacy* **1** no. 1.

Rockman, S. (2000) Laptop use and impact in the context of changing home and school access www.microsoft.com/education/?ID=AALResearch3 (Accessed 14.02.04).

Rumelhart, D.E. (1980) *Schemata: The Building Blocks of Cognition* In Spiro, R.J., Bruce, B. and Brewer W.F., (eds) *Theoretical Issues in Reading and Comprehension* Erlbaum: Hillsdale.

Sewell, D. (1990) *New Tools for New Minds* Harvester Wheatsheaf: London.

Selinger, M. (2001) *Setting Authentic Tasks Using the Internet* in Leask, M. (ed.) (2001) *Issues in Teaching Using ICT* Routledge Falmer: London.

Tann, S. (1988) *Developing Topic Work in the Primary School* Falmer Press: London.

University of Newcastle upon Tyne Department of Education (1999) *Ways Forward with ICT: Effective Pedagogy using Information and Communications Technology for Literacy and Numeracy in Primary Schools.*

Van Daal, V. and Reitsma, P. (2000) Computer-assisted learning to read and spell: results from two pilot studies. *Journal of Research in Reading,* **23** (2), 181–193.

Winkworth, E. (1977) *User Education in Schools* British Library Research and Development Department. *In* Wray and Lewis (1997).

Webquest UK, (undated) *www.webquestuk.org.uk/* (Accessed 14.02.04).

Woolfolk, A. E. (1993) *Educational Psychology,* Allyn & Bacon: Boston.

Wray, D. and Lewis, M (1997) *Extending Literacy* Routledge Falmer: London.

Index